Frontis:
The motor boat *Monarch* and the butty boat *Romford* iced up at Stenson near Derby during the early 1940s. Both boats belonged to the carrying firm of Fellows, Morton and Clayton which was undoubtedly the greatest of all the inland waterways carrying companies. Here the boatman is seen breaking up the thin ice with a pole and his wife seems to be doing the same job with a mop. Because of their considerable power the motor boats made useful ice-breaking craft with the ability to break ice up to 4in thick. The carrying firm disapproved of this practice as it could damage a boat's hull and propellor. In the last years of commercial traffic, the problem of ice was to hasten the transfer to other forms of transport. On the northern part of the canal many loads of potters materials were transferred to lorries and subsequently the traffic was lost forever.

HISTORIC WATERWAYS SCENES

THE TRENT & MERSEY CANAL

Peter Lead

Moorland Publishing

© P. Lead 1980
First published 1980
Paperback edition 1993

ISBN 0 86190 509 1

Printed in the UK by:
The Cromwell Press Ltd
Broughton Gifford, Wiltshire

Contents

Acknowledgements

The author and publisher would like to thank the following for permission to reproduce the photographs in this book: C. M. Beardmore: 119; Professor S. H. Beaver: 31-3, 38, 41, 79; Tom and Will Billings: 118; H. Bode: 105; British Rail: 23, 76; British Waterways Board: 19, 21-2, 27, 46, 86, 97; Caldon Canal Society: 85, 100, 102, 110-11; Robert Copeland: 67, 91; Mrs Olive A. Dale: 20, 25, 124; David Dyble: 74-5; *Evening Sentinel*: 26, 82, 98, 109; Gladstone Pottery Museum: 35; Dr J. R. Hollick: 87-9, 115-16, 122; William Jack: 28-30; David Jenkins: 72-3; Oswald John Lead: 2, 68; Peter Lead: 66, 70-1, 90, 101, 113; Dr Hugh Malet: 7; J. & G. Meakin: 83; Public Relations Department, Port of Manchester: 5; Manifold Collection: 12, 120-1, 125; Mrs M. Millard: 11; North Staffordshire Field Club Photographic Record: 36, 44, 99; Peter Norton: 129, 130; Hugh B. Oliver: 123, 126; Lindsey Porter: 92, 94-6, 103-4, 106-7, 112, 114, 117, 127-8, 131; BBC Hulton Picture Library: 15-16, 24; Dr J. A. Robey: 49; Frank Rogers: *frontis*, 47, 56-60, 62-5; Trustees, William Salt Library, Stafford: 4, 6; Stoke on Trent Boat Club: 43; Larry Trivett: 42; Frank Underwood, Cheddleton Flint Mill Industrial Heritage Trust: 93, (collection of the late H. C. James): 14, 17-18, 39-40, 50-5, 61, 77; Michael E. Ware: 9, 10, 34, 45, 48, 69; E. J. D. Warrillow MBE: 84; Waterways Museum, Stoke Bruerne: 13; Josiah Wedgwood & Sons Ltd: 1, 3, 8, 37, 80-1; P. Wilson: 108.

Introduction

Although by the early eighteenth century there were significant river navigations use of their upper reaches was limited by frequent shoals, meanders and constant changes in the depth and volume of their waters. The Trent was navigable as far as Nottingham throughout the seventeenth century, but efforts at improvements further upstream were blocked by determined landowners. An Act was passed in 1699 for improving the Trent Navigation from Wilden Ferry to Burton, but little seems to have been achieved and a further effort in 1714 appears to have shared the same fate. The improvements were subsequently made but even in 1766 Staffordshire merchants were complaining at the poor state of this river navigation and about the monopolists who controlled it.

The potters of North Staffordshire made use of three river navigations; china clay from Cornwall and Devon was brought by coaster to the Mersey, where it was transhipped to flats for its journey up the Weaver to Winsford and thence by waggons and packhorses to the Potteries. For the return trip the waggons and packhorses carried ware destined for Liverpool and the export market. Waggons and packhorses also made regular trips to Willington on the Trent Navigation with loads of ware for the London market, and carried back flintstones brought from the south coast through the ports of Gainsborough and Hull. Sir Richard Whitworth described the weekly traffic to Bridgnorth on the river Severn as amounting to 'about eight tons of pot ware to be conveyed to Bristol', with back loads of groceries, foreign iron and 'white clay for Burslem'.

The high costs and delays involved in transporting ware was a terrible burden to the master-potters, who were doing their utmost to be competitive. Therefore it is hardly surprising to find them amongst the most fervent supporters of the plan for a 'Staffordshire Canal'. Sir Richard Whitworth expressed their hopes when he declared that 'inland navigation will encourage old manufactures to work with fresh vigour, now their materials come cheap to them, and will give opportunity to set up new trades and manufactures as they can convey the produce or materials to any part whatsoever'. Potters figure prominently among those who shared the expense of James Brindley's 1758 survey, along with landowners like Earl Gower who were equally aware of the possibilities created by a dependable navigation. The subsequent Act makes clear the consideration that was being given to the development of Staffordshire mines and industries, as well as the untapped parts of the Cheshire saltfields.

The original impetus for the joining of the rivers Trent and Mersey came from Mr Hardman, 'an intelligent merchant of Liverpool' who organised a survey in 1755. This interest came to nothing as the Liverpool merchants busied themselves with the less ambitious Sankey Brook project and the initiative passed to the 'Staffordshire interest'. This consisted of a group of Staffordshire potters and landowners (including Earl Gower) who sponsored James Brindley to carry out a survey. There is no basis to the myth that Brindley conceived the idea of joining the two rivers, and the involvement of John Smeaton in checking and revising the proposed route indicates that the 'Staffordshire interest' had reservations about his capacity to undertake such a project.

The exact route took some time to settle, and in 1760 the plan was for the canal to run from the collieries at the southern end of Harecastle Hill through Longport to Wilden Ferry on the Trent. The original plan involving the joining of the two rivers was not revived until 1764-5 with Wedgwood and Bentley as the principal activists. Josiah Wedgwood spent a great deal of time between 1765-6 popularising the scheme and seeking the help of influential local figures. He also succeeded in protecting the yet unborn canal from the monopolistic Gower-Bridgewater interest represented by the Gilbert brothers, for it was at this time that Josiah Wedgwood asked Earl Gower in blunt terms:

> if it would not be very cruel, when a set of men had employed their time, talents & their purses for ten years together...in the execution of a design by which the Public would gain 300%, & when they have executed this laborious task — what is their reward? Why a new sett of Masters are raised up to controul both them & their works.

Their primary aims frustrated, the Gower-Bridgewater interest continued their involvement with a view to salvaging what they could, for the Duke desperately needed a northern junction between his projected canal and the one to be built between the Trent and the Mersey. In December 1765 Wedgwood expressed fears that Earl Gower might desert their cause when the Duke of Bridgewater's purposes were served and leave the eastern link unfinished. The Duke faced competition for the western link from the trustees of the Weaver Navigation who employed Robert Pownall and Hugh Henshall to survey appropriate routes in May 1765. Josiah Wedgwood negotiated with the trustees, but it seems clear that these were simply tactics devised to make the Gower-Bridgewater interest more sympathetic to the aims of the Staffordshire potters. Only at a meeting at Wolseley Bridge near Rugeley in December 1765 was the matter publicly settled, although Wedgwood and his associates had for a long time been aware how important the Gower-Bridgewater interest would be in getting the necessary parliamentary powers.

The Bill for the Trent and Mersey Canal was put before the House of Commons in February 1766 and met immediately with the anticipated and fierce opposition. The river navigations, the packhorse interests and waggoners were amongst those who combined against it, but its supporters were even more powerful and with Earl Gower's political influence the Trent and Mersey Act was passed on 14 May 1766. By an interesting coincidence the Act for the Staffordshire and Worcestershire Canal was passed on the same day. This canal was planned to run from the Trent and Mersey Canal at Great Heywood past Wolverhampton, to join the river Severn at Stourport. During the ensuing years further schemes were authorised: the Birmingham Canal (1768) to link Birmingham to the Staffordshire and Worcestershire Canal near Wolverhampton; the Coventry Canal (1768) from the Trent and Mersey at Fradley to Coventry; and the Oxford Canal (1769) which ran southwards to Oxford and the river Thames.

These subsequent developments justified the name 'Grand Trunk Canal' which was the original name given to the Trent and Mersey Canal, the idea being that the canal would form the main line of the system of canals radiating from it in various directions and linking up the greater part of the country south of the Trent to the ports of Liverpool, Hull and Bristol. Such a grand vision justified the company's patriotic motto, *Pro Patriam Populumque Fluit*, (It flows for Country and People).

The cost of Brindley's survey in 1758 and then of Smeaton's fees had been met by a subscription amongst North Staffordshire landowners (such as Earl Gower) and the potters. Thomas Whieldon and Josiah Wedgwood arranged a similar subscription in June 1765 to meet the costs of obtaining the Act of Parliament. These subscriptions ranged from modest ones of a guinea to two sums of £100 given by the Duke of Bridgewater and Earl Gower. In all something like £766 was raised by ninety-seven subscribers, the average sum subscribed being nearly £8.

Even before the Act was passed shares were being issued. Each shareholder could have a minimum of one £200 share with a maximum holding of 20 shares, although on the first issue only a William M'Guire took up a full quota of shares. The estimated cost of construction (the authorized capital) was £130,000, although the first issue, the so called 'Old Subscription' only raised £86,000. By March 1770, a 'New Subscription' had been opened and the sale of 215

further shares brought in the remaining £43,100. If this capital proved insufficient, the company was empowered to raise a further £20,000 from outside subscribers, who became proprietors or shareholders. However, early in 1770 the company secretary John Sparrow was stating that the canal would cost £200,000 to build and this was accepted by Parliament. Samuel Egerton (cousin to the Duke of Bridgewater) also lent the company £46,750 to carry on the works, to pay debts and to pay some interest to the shareholders. A further application to Parliament was necessary by 1775 and an Act passed in that year enabled the company to raise a further £75,000. Wedgwood put the total cost of building the canal at £300,000, but pointed out that 'the mere cutting of a mile of our canal would cost more than £700 or £800'.

Most of the capital came from local landowners, who contributed £141,100; and through the vigorous publicity campaign mounted by Josiah Wedgwood £56,000 was raised in London, where most of the investing public resided. North Staffordshire potters took only a modest role in financing the construction of the canal, although they realised that the success of their industry depended on it in no small measure. They subscribed the modest total of £20,000, perhaps because any large investment would have starved their businesses of much needed capital; few potters were in the enviable position of Josiah Wedgwood, who could afford to invest in the canal and a new works as well.

The test of the financial success of any canal is the dividend paid annually on the capital, and the price of shares when sold on the open market. The two tables (below) show that the Trent and Mersey Canal was in the premier league on both counts:

DIVIDEND YIELD

Year	Yield
1784	5%
1810	40%
1811	45%
1813	50%
1821	75%
1824	75% (plus bonus)
1829	75%

SHARE PRICES

Year	Value
1784	£200 at par
1792	£1000
(In 1802 the original shares of £200 were subdivided into shares of £100)	
1810	£1050
1811	£1200
1813	£1180
1821	£1810
1824	£2400
1829	£1580
1836	£2400

Brindley forecast that the canal would be completed by Christmas 1772 and was prepared to wager £200 to

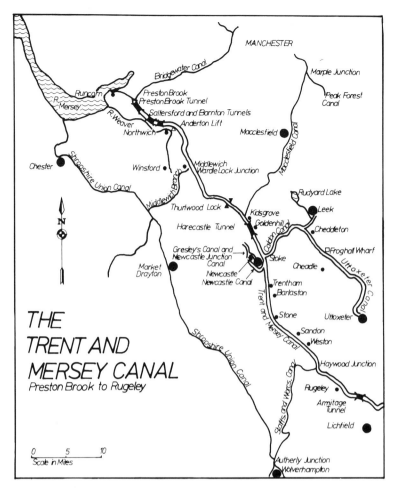

THE
TRENT AND
MERSEY CANAL
Preston Brook to Rugeley

this effect. He was probably led to believe this as cutting the canal up the valley of the Trent from its junction with the river at Derwent Mouth had proved to be relatively easy. The only significant engineering works were two aqueducts, one over the river Dove and one over the Trent at Brindley's Bank near Rugeley, and a short tunnel through easily worked rock at Armitage. Indeed the whole section of the canal south of Stoke presented few problems and was opened to traffic in October 1772.

Construction of the canal from the northern end of the summit level at Kidsgrove proved more difficult and work progressed relatively slowly. The canal was completed between Middlewich and Kidsgrove in September 1775, a section which included the thirty-five locks which take the canal down 326ft onto the Cheshire Plain. Earlier the same year, the Preston Brook Tunnel (1,239yd) was completed, enabling the section of the canal between Acton Bridge wharf and the junction with the Bridgewater Canal to be opened to traffic. The remaining length between Acton Bridge and Middlewich provided some enormous problems for Hugh Henshall. He had surveyed this part of the route himself and had originally intended to place the canal along the north side of the Weaver valley. The natural slope is very steep and the work was plagued by constant landslips and eventually Henshall was forced to tunnel at Barnton (572yd) and Saltersford (424yd).

The greatest engineering feat was doubtless the great tunnel through Harecastle Hill (2,880yd) which marked the central watershed. Some observers have wondered why a tunnel was built here at all, as a glacial meltwater channel known as the Bathpool Gap exists nearby and seemingly provides an easy and less expensive alternative, although the cost of locks or deep cuttings would have been considerable. The main reason was almost certainly one of water supply. To have used locks in the Bathpool Gap would have presented very acute problems which would have easily matched those experienced elsewhere on the national canal system. This consideration, when coupled with the knowledge that Harecastle Hill was rich in coal seams and that the workings could be drained into the canal, makes the choice of a tunnel an obvious one. When the Gilbert brothers and James Brindley created a partnership to buy the Goldenhill estate they were seeking to repeat the Worsley experiment. What they did not know was that geological conditions within the Harecastle Hill were less favourable, and hard rock and quicksand made the work excessively laborious and dangerous. Nevertheless the work was monumental in the sense that it was the first transport tunnel in England and the longest one ever attempted. Work on it was completed in April 1775 after nearly nine years of continuous effort.

The same problems were encountered when the second canal tunnel was being constructed through Harecastle Hill according to a plan prepared by Thomas Telford. The contractor Pritchard and Hoof of King's Norton reported that 'The Rock I find to be extremely hard, some of it in my opinion is much harder than ever any tunnel has been driven in before excepting the one that is executed by the side of it'. Work on this tunnel began in the summer of 1824 and was completed in April 1827, the process being greatly speeded up by cross headings driven into the earlier canal tunnel. The new tunnel was 46yd longer and 14ft in diameter, so it was wide enough to accommodate a towpath. Telford's tunnel is still in use today, unlike Brindley's which was closed because of damage caused by subsidence. At Kidsgrove the entrances still preserve their original appearance, and even a cursory examination of the two tunnels reveals the progress that had been made in the art of tunnelling in the fifty years which separate their construction.

When the canal was opened throughout in May 1777 its channel of 93 miles and the associated works made it the greatest civil engineering work so far built in England. From Derwent Mouth to Horninglow Wharf (Burton), the locks were built wide enough to enable Trent barges to reach Burton; and between Preston Brook and Middlewich the channel was of a wide gauge so that the Bridgewater vessels could reach Middlewich. A later increase in the size of these vessels meant that they could not negotiate the three western tunnels and so Preston Brook was confirmed as the transhipment point.

The locks on the Trent and Mersey are of particular interest as they are among the earliest examples of the general application of the mitre lock. Brindley had no experience of building them in December 1765 when he moved to Turnhurst Hall for sometime afterwards he built a model lock complete with gates in the grounds of his new home. In the manner of the practical mechanic he was trying out this type of lock, invented by no less a person than Leonardo da Vinci. During the present century the lock gates were removed from Turnhurst, destined for the Science Museum in London, although their present whereabouts are unknown. The brickwork of the lock was not demolished, but suffered the ignominy of being used as a rubbish dump. Should the lock be restored it could serve as a reminder of Brindley's contribution to the standardisation of lock dimensions, effecting a considerable saving in water, but recent efforts to organise a restoration programme have failed.

At Anderton (near Northwich), the Trent and Mersey Canal passes at a height of 50 ft above the River Weaver. Transhipment was carried out by an inclined plane railway from 1800, although in 1809 Telford described a proposal to build 'A Machine for raising vessels out of the river Weaver at Northwich'. The final solution to the problem was suggested by Sir E. Leader Williams, who was carrying out a series of improvements to the River Weaver in 1875, but who is best known for the remarkable swing aqueduct across the Manchester Ship Canal at Barnton. The vertical canal lift at Anderton is still an astonishing feat of engineering, and despite the heavy toll, a passage through the lift is a unique experience.

Many famous engineers worked on the Trent and Mersey and its various branches. The first one that springs to mind is James Brindley, who was appointed surveyor-general to the company in 1766, at the same time that Hugh Henshall became clerk of the works. Henshall's actual contribution remains somewhat obscure as he was not the great publicist that Brindley was, yet it is now clear that most of the detailed surveying was carried out by him as well as the cartography. He also had to supervise the actual construction work and deal with problems as they arose while Brindley was away attempting to fulfill his many commitments.

The construction of the Trent and Mersey Canal acted as a breeding ground for many early engineers. At Brindley's insistance, Joseph Parker, who was clerk of works on the Coventry Canal, spent a month with Henshall working on the Trent and Mersey. Similar arrangements were made for employees of the Oxford and Birmingham Canal Companies.

Another noted North Staffordshire canal engineer who learned his profession on the Trent and Mersey was Josiah Clowes, whose brother had married Hugh Henshall's sister. Clowes helped with the construction of the canal and spent most of his time working on the Harecastle tunnel. He later worked as a surveyor and engineer in his own right, and was associated with a number of canals, although he is best known for the construction of the tunnel at Sapperton on the Thames and Severn Canal. John Phillips, a writer on waterways and one time surveyor, claimed that he had also been involved in the construction of the canal: 'I was at the digging and vaulting of the first tunnel that ever was performed in the country, invented by my old master Mr Brindley.'

Hugh Henshall inherited Brindley's mantle as surveyor-general to the company and completed the Trent and Mersey Canal, as well as surveying the Caldon and Leek branch canals. The company also employed John Rennie as a consultant engineer until his death in 1821, and he was responsible for a variety of reports and surveys including those for the Uttoxeter Canal, the original Leek Canal and for Rudyard Lake. The company's tramroads in The Potteries and the Caldon Low tramroad are further examples of his work.

The last of the great canal engineers to be employed by the company was Thomas Telford, whose most notable works were the second Harecastle Tunnel and Knypersley Reservoir. Telford also planned the reconstruction of parts of the canal, including the duplication of locks and the straightening of the canal. Such improvements serve to demonstrate the new emphasis on speed that was necessary with the approach of the trunk railways.

Even before the completion of the main line canal, plans were being advanced for the further development and intensification of the company's system. A branch canal to Newcastle-under-Lyme had been included in the early plans for the Trent and Mersey Canal, but due to financial difficulties the scheme was shelved. This gave Sir Nigel Gresley and his son Sir Nigel Bowyer Gresley the opportunity to construct a canal from their collieries into Newcastle. Surprisingly, Sir Nigel had been declared bankrupt in 1765 and was reduced to selling his goods and Knypersley Hall, yet by 1775 he was in a position to build this canal, sharing the entire expense with his son. The canal clearly benefitted the Gresleys and as Joseph Priestley noted 'few Private works are of more real utility to the public than Sir Nigel Gresley's canal'.

The Caldon Canal was the second important development in North Staffordshire, built as the first major branch of the Trent and Mersey Canal. The Act was passed in 1776 and it empowered the canal company to build a branch canal from the Trent and Mersey Canal to Froghall and a railway from Froghall to the Cauldon Low* quarries, where there was a vast supply of limestone provided by the outcrop of Carboniferous Limestone. The canal, opened in 1778, left the main line of the Trent and Mersey at Etruria Vale and then followed an easy route, through the Stockton Brook gap and across the eastern boundary of The Potteries coalfield into the Churnet Valley. A further branch canal to Leek was constructed from the Caldon Canal under an Act of 1797, but traffic on this branch was never very significant. The Act also authorised the construction of the reservoir at Rudyard and this provided a vital supply of water which the system badly needed. In the same year another branch canal from Froghall to Uttoxeter was authorised, although various problems delayed its opening until 1811.

The agitation for a canal to Newcastle-under-Lyme was revived towards the end of the century and a branch was authorised in 1795. The canal was four miles long, starting at the junction with the Trent and Mersey Canal in Stoke and terminating on the outskirts of Newcastle. Although the canal proved a great boon to Newcastle, the major aim of the branch was frustrated as the branch was never linked with the mineral rich area to the north-west of the town. In 1798 provision was made for the construction of the Newcastle-under-Lyme Junction Canal (out of Gresley's Canal) with an inclined plane railway to join the Newcastle Canal and the Newcastle Junction Canal.

The canal was built but not the inclined plane, so the grand aim of the scheme was frustrated and this part of the coalfield was not properly developed until the coming of the railways.

The Macclesfield Canal was promoted to link the Trent and Mersey Canal with the Peak Forest Canal and received its Act in 1826. The building of the Cromford and High Peak Railway, between the Peak Forest Canal and the Cromford Canal, could well have diverted traffic from the Trent and Mersey Canal and for this reason the company supported the plan for a canal to Macclesfield, the first section of which was built as the Hall Green Branch by the Trent and Mersey Company, the whole canal being completed by 1831. Once completed this canal lessened the distance between London and Manchester by thirteen miles although with the advent of the railways this advantage was of temporary importance. The Trent and Mersey Company also built the Wardle Canal in 1829, being the first part of the Shropshire Union's Middlewich Branch, and so established a link long sought by the Chester Canal Company.

Primitive railways existed in Staffordshire as early as the seventeenth century but it was only with the coming of the canals that they acquired any real importance. The late Professor T. S. Ashton described these lines 'as feeders to the canals, rather than as an alternative means of transport', and this is generally true for the ones that existed close to the Trent and Mersey Canal. Recent research has shown how important these tramroads were, enjoying advantages in flexibility and construction costs. They were mainly concentrated on the coalfields and are more commonly associated with mines, but potteries, ironworks, quarries and mills all employed them. Most were built by private concerns, but the canal company built the Cauldon Low railways and three tramroads in The Potteries. One tramroad was even built by a separate railway company, the North Stafford or North Staffordshire Railway Company, which operated from 1815 to 1832.

The opening of the Trent and Mersey Canal and its associated canals led to quite staggering reductions in the cost of carriage, as shown by the following figures, taken from *Williamson's Liverpool Advertiser* of 8 August 1777:

COST OF GOODS TRANSPORT PER TON

Between	By Road			By Water		
	£	s	d	£	s	d
Liverpool and Etruria	2	10	0	0	13	4
" & Wolverhampton	5	0	0	1	5	0
" & Birmingham	5	0	0	1	5	0
Manchester & Wolverhampton	4	13	4	1	5	0
" & Birmingham	4	0	0	1	10	0
" & Lichfield	4	0	0	1	0	0
" & Derby	3	0	0	1	10	0
" & Nottingham	4	0	0	2	0	0
" & Leicester	6	0	0	1	10	0
" & Gainsborough	3	10	0	1	10	0
" & Newark	5	6	8	2	0	0

---

* Although there are various alternative spellings, here we will use Caldon Canal and Cauldon Low.

Clearly the cost of transport by canal was in some cases reduced to about one-quarter of the previous cost by road waggon or packhorse. Thus numerous industries in the area served by the canal obtained their raw materials much cheaper than they had done before, and secured much better facilities for distributing their goods. Ores from northern England could be brought in at less expense to mix with the poorer Staffordshire ores, and so the ironmasters were better able to deal with foreign competitors. The manufacturers of Nottingham, Derby and Leicester were afforded a cheap means of transport to the rapidly expanding port of Liverpool. Burton ales had been exported from the early part of the seventeenth century through Hull and had won renown for the Burton breweries throughout the Baltic area. It could now be conveyed by water to the port of Liverpool, to find fresh and expanding markets to the west as well as the east. The distribution of Cheshire salt was facilitated and the saltfields began to expand rapidly: production rose from 15,000 tons in 1732 to 150,000 tons in 1800. The merchants of Hull and Liverpool were also able to send groceries and other domestic supplies throughout the Midland counties much more easily, and also at reduced rates. This advantage was most obvious in the case of wheat which was conveyed for about 5s (25p) a quarter by canal, compared with £1 by road.

Of the many districts which felt the benefit of the new canal, it was the Pottery towns of North Staffordshire that received the most advantage. The construction of the canal coincided with a series of improvements in the pottery industry which heralded its movement away from coarse pottery into the production of wares of the highest quality. Great markets were available not only throughout England but throughout the World, once the old inadequate communications system was replaced by the canal. In 1760 the number of pottery workers in North Staffordshire was around 7,000 persons, many of whom according to Samuel Smiles were 'almost as rough as their roads'. The area was isolated and the people were poor and uncouth. John Wesley was laughed and jeered at when he visited Burslem in 1760, and one native even threw a clod of earth at him. Twenty-one years later he visited Burslem again and noted the changes: 'inhabitants have continually flowed in from everyside. Hence the wilderness is literally become a fruitful field. Houses, villages, towns, have sprung up, and the country is not more improved than the people.'

Much of the social improvement was due to the factory discipline imposed by Wedgwood and like minded master-potters, who were able to transform the economics of the pottery industry thanks to the opportunities presented by the new canal. Sir Richard Whitworth described how the workers had previously been 'bred up for no other use than to feed themselves' but now they could be brought into 'the world of active and productive workers'. In giving evidence to a House of Commons Committee in 1785, only eight years after the canal opened, Josiah Wedgwood stated that in The Potteries at that time from 15,000 to 20,000 workers were employed on earthenware production alone — an increase of 8,000 to 13,000 in twenty-five years. Work was easily found, and the condition of the people had been greatly improved. As the pottery factories multiplied and grew in size, so did the coal mines and the influx of colliers must have at least matched that of the potters. The canal also heralded the last great phase in the North Staffordshire iron industry which had been declining steadily throughout the eighteenth century but was revived by the introduction of coke fired furnaces in 1785.

The list of tolls charged during the months June to September 1783 gives some idea of the goods carried during the early stages of commercial activity. Earthenware was the most important traffic, followed by potters' materials and then the traffic in lime and limestone:

Goods carried	Tolls Paid
Earthenware	£587
Clay	£541
Lime and Limestone	£515
Grain, Meal, Flour	£456
Salt	£326
Harecastle Coal	£296
Timber	£259
Flint	£249
Iron	£184
Groceries	£158
Nails	£89
Cheese	£72

Detailed records of total trade on the Trent and Mersey Canal are difficult to locate, but information is available for long distance trade in and out of The Potteries for the year ending 30 June 1836. Inward trade totalled 143,610 tons, consisting of 129,800 tons from the Mersey; including 70,000 tons of clay and stone from Devon, Dorset and Cornwall; 30,000 tons of flint and 4,000 tons of other potters materials; 8,260 tons from South Staffordshire, 7,000 tons of which was iron; 3,500 tons from London and 2,500 tons from Manchester. Outward trade totalled 184,500 tons; of which 61,000 tons went to Liverpool, made up of 51,000 tons of earthenware and china, and 10,000 tons of bricks and tiles; 59,000 tons to Manchester, including 3,500 tons of earthenware and china, 30,000 tons of bricks and tiles, and 25,000 tons of coal for Manchester and Stockport; 15,000 tons of calcined ironstone to South Staffordshire; 6,000 tons of earthenware and china to Birmingham and the west of England; 12,000 tons of earthenware and china, and 30,000 tons of coal to London; and 1,000 tons of earthenware and china to Chester and North Wales.

Obviously this should not be taken as a complete picture of trade on the Trent and Mersey Canal, nor should it be taken as representative of the earlier phase of the canal's history. For instance the trade in coal to Manchester and Stockport only became viable when the Macclesfield Canal was opened. The figures do not deal with local trade, or the important limestone trade, at a time when the Cauldon Low quarries were producing between 65,000 and 100,000 tons annually. Salt is also excluded and despite the continued importance of the Weaver Navigation the canal carried a large proportion of the total production of the Cheshire saltfields. The whole of the production of the Shirleywich saltworks (near Stafford), some 12,500 tons a year, was carried on the canal; as well as the 16,000 tons of coal used annually at the works.

The coal working area around Rugeley and Brereton was given a new lease of life by the construction of the canal, which was linked to the collieries by tramroads. By the 1840s Brereton Colliery was probably producing 60,000 tons a year. Few settlements along the canal can owe so much to it as Kidsgrove, which developed its collieries under the stimulus of the new markets provided by the canal. As early as 1800 a traveller, the Reverend Richard Warner, noted 'the destruction of all its picturesque beauty by the introduction of the black and nasty apparatus accompanying coal mines, several of which, belonging to a Mr Gilbert, are worked to a depth of five hundred and forty feet.'

Initially the carrying trade on the canal was in the hands of a few private carriers and private individuals. One of the earliest was the Cavendish Boat Company, who unfortunately went bankrupt in 1781 when they were operating twenty boats on the canal. Another firm of carriers was Hugh Henshall and Company, who were in fact controlled by the canal company itself. Other major Staffordshire operators in 1795 included: the Burton Boat Company (18 boats); John Gilbert (16 boats); J. Smith and Sons, of Burton (13 boats); Charles Moore, of Shirleywich Saltworks (8 boats); William Kenwright and Company, of Stoke (7 boats); and Parker and Company of Apedale ironworks (8 boats). At this time 211 boats were registered along the Trent and Mersey Canal in Staffordshire, including one to a boatwoman, Elizabeth Marsh of Colton.

As The Potteries were in the words of John Ward 'at the heart of the Grand Trunk', it is informative to determine which carriers were operating wharves there in the late 1830s. Hugh Henshall and Company were the principal carriers, although Henshall himself had died in 1817. By this time the Anderton Company was well represented; along with Messrs T. and M. Pickford; George Appleby and Company; James Sutton and Company; Heath and Son; Morris, Herbert and Company; Kenworthy and Company; Mills and Company; and Ebbern and Sons. There had been many others too numerous to mention here, but it should be noted that the label '& Co' may well have been a loose expression, used to describe the affairs of two humble boatmen owning one boat in partnership. Colliery and iron companies owned their own boats, like the seven boats operated by John Sparrow (clerk to the company) from the Cockshead Colliery on the Caldon Canal.

Passenger services never appear to have been organised on the Trent and Mersey Canal in the way they were on some other canals. Any potential traveller had to make their own arrangements with the boat's captain and presumably haggle over the fare. One such traveller was Christina Collins who set out by canal in 1839 to journey from Liverpool to London where her husband had just found a new job. After reaching Preston Brook by the fly boat service along the Bridgewater Canal, she boarded a Pickford's boat for the remainder of the journey, which included part of the Trent and Mersey Canal. Soon she noticed that the captain and the crew seemed to have an insatiable craving for drink and an unwelcome interest in herself. As the boat made its way down the canal, the situation worsened until, between Colwich and Rugeley, she was raped and then pushed into the water to drown. The crew were apprehended and subsequently the captain and a member of the crew were hanged at Stafford. This case did nothing to improve the image of boatmen and also added substance to the growing legend of the 'Kidsgrove Boggart'.

The canal was also used during the Irish Rebellion of 1798 to convey troops to Ireland, and it may also be surmised that other troops were transported in this way during the Napoleonic Wars.

The boats used by the long distance carriers were of a light, all timber construction, with fine lines at the stem and stern, and a pronounced roundness in the hull section. They were built with a cabin at the rear and few changes were made to the design in the 150 years that they served on the canal. Limited modifications were introduced with the coming of the railways, when it became necessary to make the boats more suitable for the transport of bulk cargoes. Josiah Wedgwood described the dimensions of the boats used on 'our canal' as being '70 feet long by 7 in breadth'.

In another document written by Josiah Wedgwood in 1786, and now preserved in the University of Keele, he describes a boat he wanted building. It was to be 68ft long at the bottom and 6ft 10in wide 'from outside to outside'. It was also to have a 'false bottom' to be laid 'crossways at the Foredeck' to prevent water entering the boat as it passed through locks. The boat was to have a cabin with 'bedsides and two cupboards besides the stern cupboard and two shelves'. For such a boat Wedgwood was prepared to pay 14½ guineas (roughly £15.25); and presumably it was built, for one boat was registered to 'Wedgwood & Co, Etruria' in 1795. How realistic Wedgwood's estimate was can be judged from the fact that in 1796 the Cheddleton Lime Company paid £90 for a similar boat.

Tub boats were considered for use on the projected Caldon Canal in 1773, when a system of inclined planes was being considered instead of locks. These boats were seen as being capable of carrying anything between 5 and 8 tons, and the system had it been built would have been like that being built by Davies Ducart on the Tyrone Navigation at the same time. Boats like tub boats were used in the Harecastle Tunnel for maintenance purposes, but these were essentially work flats. Smaller boats were used in the Harecastle workings to bring coal from the coalface, but there are no details of their construction although it would be reasonable to suppose that they owed something to the Worsley starvationers.

The origin of the canal boatmen still remains unclear, but it is likely that many of them were recruited from the original workforce engaged in the construction of the canal. Some worked exclusively for the carrying companies, such as Hugh Henshall and Company, Worthington and Gilbert, and Pickfords, while others operated their own boats and sometimes subcontracted to the carrying companies. Most had houses near the canal and one Isaac Jones of Lawton owned six houses at the time of his death. They were relatively prosperous workers until the coming of the railways, when trade became less lucrative and they were forced by economic pressures to live on their boats.

An interesting biography of a boatman has been recently unearthed. The account deals with the life of Joseph Bowyer who was born at Stanley in 1818, and died at Brown Edge in 1903. He was the son of Samuel Bowyer, himself a boatman, and at first he worked with his father boating limestone from Froghall to Longport with the odd trip into South Staffordshire. When Joseph was sixteen years of age his father died and he took charge of the boat, carrying on the trade in limestone from Froghall as before. Three years later he was hired to take his boat to Paddington canal wharf (London), where he was to load some carved stone for the new hall being built at Trentham by the Duke of Sutherland. He continued in this work for seven years, boating stone and other materials from various parts of the country to Trentham Hall. Stone flags from Yorkshire and slates from North Wales made up some of his loads. After this he rather ironically had a hand in building the Grand Junction Railway, for he spent a time boating the original stone sleepers on which the rails were laid. Later he returned to the Froghall limestone trade, ultimately ending his working career as a boatman for Richard Deane, who owned one of the Norton collieries.

The Act laid down that there were to be two bodies: the company of shareholders of the Trent and Mersey Canal and 816 commissioners who were to 'settle, determine and adjust all questions, matters and differences', which might arise between the company and the people affected by the construction of the canal. An executive committee was formed in June 1766 when key officers were elected in the presence of most of the shareholders.

By 1776, the committee was made up of fourteen members with a pronounced group of six centred on the two Gilbert brothers, linked by marriage and

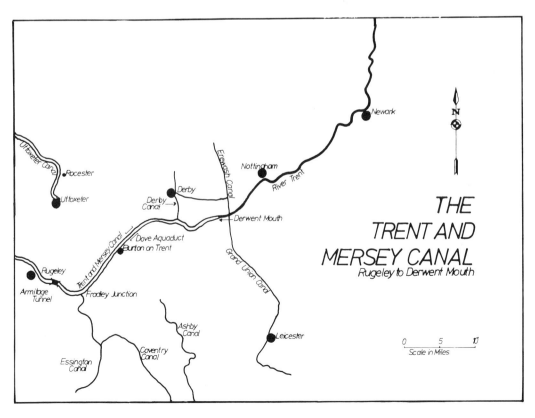

THE TRENT AND MERSEY CANAL
Rugeley to Derwent Mouth

business interests. This division within the committee became very obvious in 1783-5 when the very stability of the company was threatened. John Gilbert had formed a company of canal carriers in 1782 known as Worthington and Gilbert, which operated in opposition to Hugh Henshall and Company. Not surprisingly, the Duke of Bridgewater's trade went to Gilbert, whose boats also received preferential treatment on the Bridgewater Canal, when it came to loading and unloading. A row broke out in committee which promptly split into two groups; one headed by Josiah Wedgwood, and the other the Gilbert faction with Thomas Gilbert to the fore. Pamphlets flew backwards and forwards, one issued by Thomas Gilbert being particularly damaging, as he claimed that the committee's affairs were 'totally deranged'. The matter dragged on for several years, the potters being determined that the Duke of Bridgewater should no longer treat their canal as a branch of his own, and eventually the Duke induced the Gilberts to back down. After this the Gilberts faded out of the affairs of the company although they remained as shareholders.

The head office of the company was established in Westbridge House, Stone, which was also the home of the company's chief agent. This post carried responsibility for the smooth running and maintenance of the canal. He was charged with enforcing the company's regulations and bye-laws, and to help him in his task he had assistants like Joseph Popplewell who was 'clerk of the cheque office, near Etruria' in 1818. These clerks were stationed at various points along the canal and they dealt with the waybills that every boat captain had to carry. The company also employed 'Walking Surveyors' who patrolled the canal on foot and were in Wedgwood's words 'the Ears and Eyes for the Committee, that is, for the Proprietors at large', in short their work was largely that of the policeman.

The company also employed lock-keepers; clerks and labourers for their warehouses; as well as a wide range of craftsmen and labourers who maintained the canal and associated works. New works were generally undertaken by outside contractors due to their scale.

By the 1840s the Trent and Mersey Canal Company had realised that railway competition could not be held off indefinitely. On one side they had the Grand Junction Railway and on the other the Midland Railway, not to mention the host of railway schemes that were being hatched to serve North Staffordshire itself. Following the example of canal companies elsewhere in the kingdom, the company decided that they would try and sell themselves to the infant North Staffordshire Railway Company. Under the terms of the railway Acts of 1846 and 1847 the canal was merged with the railway company and the canal capital converted into 5 per cent preference railway shares worth £1,170,000.

The railway company considered the canal as a feeder, so it did not initially desire to phase out the canal trade. Three of the nine railway directors were obliged to become canal directors, and at various times the railway company undertook to maintain the canal. By the 1860s the effect of railway competition was beginning to show, and it necessitated reductions in canal tolls in an effort to maintain the existing traffic. A gradual decline in both tonnage and tolls continued throughout the remaining years of the century.

As the Trent and Mersey Canal served as an importing and exporting route for The Potteries, the proportion of non-local traffic remained far higher than was the case on most canals at this time. Total traffic declined from 1,139,098 tons in 1888 to 1,215,540 tons in 1898 and 1,137,663 tons in 1905. Included in this last figure was 374,387 tons of local traffic. A normal week's traffic included coal 5,500 tons, potters materials 4,000 tons, limestone 2,500 tons, salt 2,000 tons, earthenware 1,000 tons, manufactured iron 500 tons, iron ore 200 tons, and sundries (including flour and grain) 7,000 tons.

During the present century the decline on the Trent and Mersey Canal continued. The causes included the closing of important collieries and ironworks in North Staffordshire, continuing railway competition, new competition from road transport and reducing coal freight resulting from the increasing use of oil and electricity. The old method of stimulating trade by reducing tolls resulted in reduced receipts, and so offered no real solution to the problem. A picture of the decline in the traffic on the canal emerges from the following annual tonnage figures for the Trent and Mersey:

Year	Annual Tonnage Carried
1905	1,137,663
1912	1,059,035
1924	534,821
1930	423,276
1938	385,870
1946	186,670
1952	132,738
1959	23,940
1963	12,399

Clearly by the early 1960s, commercial traffic on the canal was slight and road and rail transport had triumphed. At the same time the canal was experiencing a kind of renaissance because of the growing interest in pleasure craft, which has grown steadily ever since. One encouraging development has been the introduction of specially designed craft by Johnson Brothers, to carry ware from their factories in Hanley to their packing house at Milton, four miles away on the Caldon Canal. From time to time attempts are made to reintroduce commercial traffic to the canal, but in the present economic situation the chances of success are slight.

A number of quite serious attempts have been made for reviving commercial traffic on the canal, including a proposal to supply Meaford power station (near Stone) with coal. Tom Wilson has pointed out that to deliver the 9,000 tons of coal needed weekly at the power station would require the weekly arrival of some 450 narrow boats, far more than ever passed Meaford when canal traffic was at its height!

The Canal Promoters

1   Inspired by the success of the Duke of Bridgewater's first canal, Josiah Wedgwood took the initiative in revitalising a ten-year-old scheme to join the River Mersey to the River Trent. In the years 1765-6, he spent a great deal of his time popularising the canal scheme and soliciting the help of influential local figures. He also succeeded in protecting the canal from the monopolistic interests represented by the two Gilbert brothers; he was in favour of a more democratic governing body. At the first meeting of the company in June 1766 he was appointed treasurer, earning (as he termed it) 'a salary of £0,000 per annum'. This appointment was very important to the Staffordshire Potteries, for they secured the man in charge of the purse strings, as well as an active proprietor who went up and down the canal almost as much as the various engineers.

2   Thomas Whieldon (1719-95) was in his time the most prominent of the Staffordshire potters and during 1754-9 he had Josiah Wedgwood as his junior partner. Because of his local importance, it is hardly surprising to find him as chief amongst the 'other gentlemen' who shared in the expenses of Brindley's 1758 survey. He was joint treasurer with Wedgwood of the fund to promote the Act of Parliament authorising the canal, to which they contributed 10 and 5 guineas respectively. After this his involvement in the affairs of the company became less marked, although he held shares worth £2,500. In April 1775 he constructed at his own expense a wharf and basin at what is now Whieldon's Grove, Stoke, where the Newcastle to Uttoxeter turnpike road crossed the canal. This was intended to handle the Fenton and Longton trade, his own works being nearby at Little Fenton.

3   The original idea for a Trent and Mersey canal had been produced by a group of Liverpool merchants, who had commissioned a survey in 1755. The engineers they employed were William Taylor and John Eyes, who reported in favour of the scheme. No further action was taken, however, mainly because both the merchants and the engineers became involved in the promotion and construction of the Sankey Navigation. Thomas Bentley (1731-80), best known as Josiah Wedgwood's partner, belonged to this community of merchants and he probably interested Wedgwood in the scheme. They first met in 1760 and by April 1765, Wedgwood was writing to him 'to draw his quill for the service of his Country'. The result was the now famous pamphlet which outlined the advantages of the proposed canal and doubtless played an invaluable part in obtaining parliamentary powers.

1

2

3

4 As brother-in-law to the Duke of Bridgewater, it seems especially appropriate that Earl Gower should have shared his interest in canals. In 1758, Earl Gower, Lord Anson, Thomas Broade and a number of 'other gentlemen' commissioned James Brindley to survey the route of the proposed canal; this was reviewed three years later by John Smeaton. Earl Gower was the most influential figure in Staffordshire at that time, as well as being a national political force. When he pledged his support for the canal scheme at the open-air meeting at Wolseley Bridge in December 1765 it was the signal for the local landed gentry to follow suit. Josiah Wedgwood had reservations about the Earl's true motives and at one time felt he might only be interested in forming a junction with the Duke of Bridgewater's canal.

5 Francis Egerton, third Duke of Bridgewater, was the un-doubted founder of British inland navigation by canal. He was also the employer of the two Gilbert brothers and, for a while, of James Brindley. The duke was an unusually enlightened employer and a firm believer in the creed of public rather than private benefit. His motives, however, were sometimes suspected, especially by the Staffordshire potters who feared a canal dominated by the Gower-Bridgewater interest. The duke was keen to have the northern end of the Trent and Mersey canal join his canal from Manchester to Runcorn, and went to a lot of trouble to achieve this aim. This interest occasioned him to buy shares worth £4,000, at a time when he was desperately short of capital. His patronage and involvement helped the canal company tremendously, although he appears sometimes to have treated the Trent and Mersey as a branch of his own canal.

6 Thomas Gilbert was employed as a legal adviser and agent by both the Duke of Bridgewater and Earl Gower; on their behalf he spearheaded the abortive attempt to gain control of the proposed canal. As Member of Parliament for Newcastle-under-Lyme he was able to steer the canal bill through Parliament, and he was chairman of the parliamentary committee which considered it after its second reading. He was probably the first chairman of the canal company committee, a position he still held in 1776 as the main line neared completion. Thomas Gilbert held shares in the company worth £4,000, a holding equal to that of his two masters, whose interests he repre-sented on the committee. He was involved in the early attempts to promote the Coventry Canal, and was a major shareholder in the Shrewsbury and Shropshire Canals.

7 John Gilbert, younger brother to Thomas, was the chief agent on the Duke of Bridgewater's estate at Worsley in Lancashire. Modern research has shown that he was an exceptionally gifted canal and mining engineer, and that he was responsible for a number of major works previously credited to James Brindley. His role in the construction of the Bridgewater Canals has been ably documented, but his involvement with other canals is only now coming to light. He held a considerable number of shares in the Trent and Mersey Canal, although Josiah Wedgwood had to wait for some time before Gilbert actually paid for them. In 1782 his firm of Worthington and Gilbert were at the centre of an argument over preferential treatment on the Duke's canal, and this split the Trent and Mersey committee into two groups and threatened the stability of the company.

8 James Brindley's true genius has been greatly distorted by a multitude of historians whose view of him has been coloured by the writings of Samuel Smiles. He was an undoubted master of water supply and control, although his grasp of certain other technical matters was not always what it should have been. His involvement with the Fenton steam engines and his experimental locks at Turnhurst all point towards greater abilities as a 'schemer' rather than as an engineer. He surveyed the route of the canal from the River Trent to Longport in 1758, only to have his work checked and revised by John Smeaton. As 'Surveyor General' to the canal company he drew a salary of £200, a figure nearly double that given to Hugh Henshall as 'Clerk of Work'. Henshall made a greater contribution to the construction of the canal than did Brindley, including the survey for the whole section between Harecastle Hill and Preston Brook.

The Main Line

9

9 The Anderton Company boat *Thames* seen after unloading at Bottom Locks, Runcorn about 1910. The company built its own boats at Middleport and they had a number of distinctive features including low cabins, which eased the difficulties of negotiating Brindley's Harecastle tunnel. These boats carried crated earthenware from the Potteries to Runcorn in loads seldom exceeding five or six tons because of the bulky nature of the cargo.

Return loads for the boats included a wide range of potters' materials for the company's wharves at Port Vale (Longport) and Etruria Vale, as well as to the numerous private wharves along the canal. The company came into existence in 1836 to take over the transhipment traffic at Anderton and even managed to retain something of its identity after it was taken over by the Mersey Weaver and Ship Canal Company in 1954.

10

11

10   There are three tunnels on the Trent and Mersey canal in Cheshire, at Saltersford, Barnton and Preston Brook. There was no towpath through any of them, and so the boats had to be legged through; thus as traffic increased so did the delays. The North Staffordshire Railway and Canal Company decided in 1864 to remedy the situation by introducing tunnel tugs. The effect of the smoke on the crews in the following boats is easily imagined and it was not unknown for crews to be overcome by fumes, which resulted in one fatal accident at Preston Brook in 1865, before the four air shafts were completed. Due to the primitive techniques of the early engineers, this tunnel had a slight 'S' bend in it and to assist the tug's passage it was fitted with spring-loaded arms with two sets of guide wheels which ran along the tunnel wall, so making steering unnecessary. This photograph shows a train of boats entering Saltersford tunnel in 1910 accompanied by clouds of smoke.

11   This is the Preston Brook tug at the northern end of the tunnel, and the guide wheels are clearly seen. There was one tug at each of the three Cheshire tunnels with one in reserve; they maintained a 50-minute service backwards and forwards from 6.00am to 8.30pm until about 1943 when few horse boats were left.

12   The North Staffordshire Railway and Canal Company built and maintained at least one of their canal tugs at their central workshops. This rare picture was taken at Stoke in 1865 and it shows the newly constructed Barnton tug. Although tugs were not employed until this time there had been a practical demonstration of their potential on the Trent and Mersey canal as early as 1828. An inventor called David Gordon made a trip from Paddington to Manchester in 'a steam-vessel, built for the purpose of navigating the canals of the kingdom; an attempt which has been once or twice made, but has never heretofore succeeded.' At Preston Brook this vessel towed a large boat laden with timber through the tunnel; 'thus saving the labour usual in passing through tunnels, and which is most unfriendly to the health and safety of the labourers [leggers] employed in that task.' Wisely, nothing was said at this time about the dangers from smoke and fumes.

13 The chutes used for the transhipment of salt are well in evidence in this photograph of the Anderton lift, which connected the River Weaver and the Trent and Mersey Canal and is shown here in its original state. Designed by Edwin Clark the lift opened in 1875 and consisted of two tanks or 'caissons' supported on hydraulic rams in equilibrium, and so one tank was always up and the other down. When in use the boat and cargo float into one of the tanks either above or below, or when possible both contain boats. The gates, closing the ends of the tanks, would then also be closed and the machine set in motion by withdrawing a small amount of water from the lower tank. The extra weight of the descending tank then caused them to change places, the ascending boat being transferred through 50ft to the canal and the descending boat to the river.

14

15

14 A small hydraulic pump made up the losses by friction and other mechanical causes, but five-sixths of the transfer was performed by the slight difference in weight of water in the tanks. The tanks were designed to accommodate two narrow boats, or one large barge (known as 'dukers' to the locals) of up to 100 tons. The weight of each tank, including water and ironwork, is 252 tons, which never changes for the boat displaces its own weight of water. This rare photograph shows the lower end of the lift in close-up and was taken about 1903. The engine house and chimney can be seen to the right of the photograph. After working for nearly thirty years it was found that considerable repairs were necessary and more especially to the main rams, upon which the whole weight of 252 tons was balanced.

15 In order to repair or renew the main rams, a stoppage for a considerable time would have been necessary, but it was vital not to interrupt the flow of traffic between the river and the pottery district. Eventually it was decided to suspend the caissons by wire ropes onto an overhead arrangement of wheels and pulleys with counterweights at the other end of the ropes, similar to an ordinary window sash. A clear idea of the principle comes from thinking of a large number of window sashes fastened securely together, each one having its own pulleys and counter-weights. The essential difference, however, between the window frame and the arrangement of the lift is that the power is applied directly to the pulleys through suitable gearing, so that they are all made to revolve together and thus raise or lower the mass.

16 By adopting this method, the repairs and alterations were carried out with only three stoppages of about a fortnight each and the reconstructed lift opened on 29 July 1908. This made obsolete the necessity for hydraulic power, as an electric motor was more convenient for operating the pulleys, and there was also the great advantage that all parts of the machinery were above ground and easily access-ible. There was practically no maintenance, except to see that the ropes were not stranding, in which case it was quite easy to renew them one at a time. The alterations made the transit of boats a more rapid process and also reduced the power costs. The lift is situated on an island in the basin of the river and it was necessary to build an aqueduct to carry the canal to it, as can be seen from this photograph.

17

18

17 On the 21 July 1907 the Trent and Mersey Canal burst its banks north of the Forge Brook culvert at Marbury. The canal suffered considerably from subsidence in this area due to the old rock salt mines, which were badly eroded by water leaking into them from Forge Brook. A period of heavy rain was sufficient to complete the process and a short length of the canal bank collapsed. This view shows a maintenance crew working in the breach. Apart from an interesting collection of tools, it is also possible to detect pieces of the first brine pipeline which crossed the canal at this point; this pipeline was constructed in 1882 by the Mersey Salt and Brine Company and it was to be the cause of much friction with the North Staffordshire Railway Company, who foresaw the loss of their salt trade.

18 The second photograph shows the breach and two narrow boats that, in the words of one observer: 'rushed down with the water but stuck on the bottom'. Another boat, which also came to grief because of the burst, was carrying a load of cheeses from Nantwich to Runcorn. When the owners arrived to check the load, they noticed that the number of cheeses had diminished considerably, although none of the locals could help with their enquiries. This event just happened to coincide with a drop in the local demand for cheese which lasted for several weeks. The picture also shows a small tramway which carried coal from a staithe to a nearby pumping station belonging to the Salt Union; in 1888 this company had taken over the brine pipeline which ran between Marston and Weston Point.

19 Due to the acute nature of the subsidence in the Marston-Witton area, a new stretch of canal 1,750ft long was built to avoid a particularly troublesome tract of land. The photograph shows it at the time of its opening on 19 May 1958 and the original line of the canal can still be seen behind the bulldozer. It was in the Marston area that an important breakthrough was made in 1780 or 1781, when the lower or main bed of rock salt was discovered. The engineer was John Gilbert, a proprietor of the canal company and a shareholder in the Marston saltworks. He installed a Boulton and Watt rotative steam engine around 1788 for winding salt out of the pit and for pumping brine as well. At the same time the mine was producing at least 12,000 tons of salt a year, all of which was carried away on the canal.

20 The canal was very important to the Cheshire salt industry as it extended communications by water into other parts of Cheshire and the Trent Valley, notably with the North Staffordshire coalfield from which coal was carried to the refineries and later to the chemical industry. In the 1890s chlorine and caustic soda began to be produced by the electrolysis of brine. Hargreaves and Bird began this type of production at Farnworth and, following the success of their pilot plant, formed the General Electrolytic Alkali Company with a works at Cledford Bridge near Middlewich, where production began in 1899. The photograph shows the Cledford Bridge works about 1905 when it made considerable use of the canal; coal was brought in by boat and various alkalis were taken away by canal, although the works were also served by a spur line from the LNWR.

21 The entrance to the two locks at Thurlwood near Rode Heath as they were in 1955. This photograph clearly shows how acute the problem of subsidence was in this area. The double-arched bridge which formerly spanned the lower ends of the lower locks had already been demolished and replaced by a temporary wooden bridge, which in turn was replaced by a bridge made of pre-stressed concrete. Adjacent to these locks is the site of Lawton saltworks, established in 1779; these works were later flooded, and salt pumping substituted for mining. After pumping had ceased in 1927, the nearby River Wheelock changed its course, and part of it flowed down the shaft, causing the acute subsidence that increasingly affected the canal. Faced with the imminent collapse of both locks the British Waterways Board came up with an enterprising solution in the form of a prefabricated steel tank lock.

21

22 This photograph shows the new lock a few weeks before it was opened on 19 May 1958. One of the locks remained in use while the other was stripped of its masonry and brickwork, and a concrete retaining wall built as a support. This lock is 106ft long and 12ft 6in high with an inside width of 7ft 9in, and is supported on concrete piers placed 8ft apart. Each pier is equipped with two jacking points so that it can be raised to its original level should further subsidence occur. The gears for the gates and sluices are operated in the normal way with a windlass, but the gates are of the guillotine type and the lock is filled through steel pipes attached to the sides of the tank. Although it is a superb piece of engineering it has been little used as it takes much longer to fill than the adjacent conventional lock.

23   The 'ginny system' was designed by John Curr to make the transportation of coal from the coal-face to the wharf into one smooth operation. Underground the coal was loaded into waggons and conveyed to the base of the shaft where chains were attached to haul them to the surface. Here they would be placed back on the tramroad track and conveyed to the canalside wharf. Taken near Church Lawton in 1895, this photograph shows the tramroad from Bunkers Hill Colliery, just above the canal wharf which lay on the far side of the bridge. Note the plate rails and ginny waggons (known in this pit as 'nibbles') with the iron eyes to which the chains were attached. This system was introduced to the North Staffordshire Coalfield by John Gilbert who used it about 1792, to connect his Kidsgrove mines with the canal.

24   This print was published in 1785 and is clearly the work of a romanticist as it bears no relation to the real situation. It does, however, convey a great deal about the spirit of the time and the way in which the Harecastle Tunnel grasped the public imagination. Before the construction of the tunnel the only comparable works were drainage adits or soughs opened into mines. Boats were kept for the purpose of showing visitors the tunnel and one such visitor described it as 'our eighth wonder of the world'. Another visitor was struck by 'the view back upon the mouth, like the glimmering of a star, very beautiful'. Sir Joseph Banks visited the southern heading of the tunnel late in 1767 and seems to have been impressed with it, although he found the mortar soft and feared that the tunnel might collapse. His companion John Gilbert must have thought of Brindley's problems with the Barton aqueduct.

25   Contrary to the fears of Sir Joseph Banks, the Harecastle Tunnel had a long and useful life and this photograph shows J. & G. Meakin's *Westwood* entering it, around 1905. Almost as soon as the tunnel opened it became obvious that it was a bottle-neck and special rules were devised for passing through it. Boats were only allowed to begin their passages at specified times and they were allowed 3 hours to reach the other end; failure to comply resulted in a fine of £5. The problem was made even worse by the lateral tunnels which served the mines and along which coal and ironstone were conveyed in tub boats. One of the tunnels ran to the Goldenhill Ironworks which stood astride a shaft rather like the Butterley Ironworks in Derbyshire. James Brindley, John Brindley, Hugh Henshall, and Thomas and John Gilbert, all had an interest in these mines.

23

24

25

LEGGING. TUNNEL. HAREGASTLE.

26 A view of the northern end of the Harecastle tunnels taken in the late 1940s. Telford's tunnel is to the left and the overhead cable for the electric tug can be clearly seen. The moored narrow boat was designed to block the approach to Brindley's tunnel, seen to the right, while the other two craft were used for maintenance purposes in Brindley's tunnel, which although disused by this time still needed considerable attention. The tub-shaped boat is essentially a work flat, but the other boat is of considerable interest. Smaller boats were used in the side tunnels to reach the coal workings, in the way the famous 'starvationers' were used at Worsley, and one local source stated that the Harecastle boats were not unlike the one shown in this photograph. The appearance of the boatman on the planking helps to explain why many regarded the boatpeople as 'water gipsies'.

27 An obvious solution to the problem was to build a second tunnel, but the canal company shied away from this proposal, mindful of the cost and difficulties involved in building the first tunnel. John Rennie recommended a new tunnel in 1820, but it was only the threat of competition from the Shropshire Union Canal which spurred the company into taking positive action. They called in Thomas Telford as consultant engineer and work began in February 1825 and was completed on 16 March 1827, having cost £112,681. During the construction a double-track tramroad had been laid over Harecastle Hill which speeded up the construction work and helped to ease the traffic problem. Telford's tunnel was larger in section than the old one and included a towpath which alone cost £9,600. This unique photograph shows this towpath being removed in 1974.

28 In the North Staffordshire Railway Act 1904, the company obtained powers to use 'tugs worked by electricity or mechanical power other than steam', in the Harecastle Tunnels. Because of local opposition, the company were not able to establish the service until November 1914 when an electric tug was bought for use in Telford's tunnel. The original system involved the tugs dragging themselves along a steel cable which ran along the bed of the tunnel. The cable passed over two winding drums mounted in the tugs and operated by a 15hp electric motor. There was no other means of steering. Power was obtained from an accumulator barge which was towed behind the tug and contained 115 chloride cells. This photograph shows one of the tugs emerging from the Kidsgrove end of the tunnel in 1953, by which time both the tugs and the system had been considerably modified.

29 The original system worked well and by early 1915 it was handling nearly two hundred boats daily, working an 18-hour day. Brindley's tunnel was finally abandoned in 1918 and so the use of the tugs became compulsory for boats wishing to negotiate the tunnel. The charge for haulage through Harecastle was 6d (2½p) per boat empty or laden up to 2 tons, or 1s (5p) per boat laden above 2 tons. In 1931 a major change was made to the system when the accumulator boats were discarded and power supplied by a cable fixed to the tunnel roof. Current was collected in a similar manner to a tramcar as this photograph (also taken in 1953) shows. The second tug is moored against the right-hand bank. Unfortunately by 1950 traffic had become so slight that it was no longer economic to maintain the tug service and they were allowed to fall into disrepair.

30 By January 1953 the Docks and Inland Waterways Executive authorised a scheme to install a system of forced ventilation in Telford's tunnel to enable boats to pass through the tunnel under their own power. A building was constructed across the tunnel mouth at Chatterley to accommodate three 38 in diameter fans. Here the building is shown as it neared completion in 1954. Both the tunnels through Harecastle Hill have suffered badly from subsidence and in September 1973 two roof-falls forced the closure of Telford's tunnel, and only then did the true extent of the problem come to light. Due to the terrible conditions and the extent of the damage, it took three and a half years to complete repairs. The tunnel was re-opened on 2 April 1977 by Sir Frank Price.

31 A view of Goldendale Ironworks taken in 1950 showing the blast furnaces, offices and one of the saddle-tank engines used for shunting around the works. The Goldendale furnaces opened in 1840 on a site just to the south of the Harecastle Tunnels and at that time the canal was its sole means of communication. During the construction of Telford's tunnel the site was used for manufacturing bricks and preparing mortar for use in building the new tunnel. Two steam engines, including one by Boulton and Watt, had been employed on the site. It also marked one terminus of the tramroad over Harecastle Hill, part of which was relaid by Robert Williamson between Goldenhill and the Goldendale site in 1827. This line brought down calcined ironstone which was forwarded by canal to blast furnaces in South Staffordshire and Wales. When the Goldendale ironworks opened it received its raw materials along this tramroad.

32 The Mersey, Weaver and Ship Canal Carrying Company operated a fleet of about seventy boats at its peak, although by 1939 the number was nearer fifty. The company were formed in the late nineteenth century as a subsidiary of the Salt Union and remained under their control until 1935 when the Union was absorbed by Imperial Chemical Industries. At the time of the merger, the Mersey Weaver carrying fleet was bought by its manager, C. W. Shirley, and remained in the hands of the Shirley family until 1958 when it was bought by British Waterways. The company carried a wide range of cargoes from Weston Point or Runcorn to the Potteries. Deliveries of potters' materials were made primarily to the company's own wharves at Longport and to their Colonial Wharf at Brownhills near Tunstall. This photograph shows the Colonial Wharf during the

summer of 1950 when regular deliveries were still being made.

33 Longbridge (now Longport) was to be the terminal point of the canal from the River Trent which Brindley surveyed in February 1758. A wharf here would have served Burslem and

Tunstall and completed the link of the pottery towns with Hull. This photograph, taken in 1950, shows a pottery at Longport (demolished in 1962) with several characteristic 'bottle-kilns' and a wharf for landing clay from the canal.

34 Taken at Middleport in the early years of this century, this photograph shows the large covered boatyard owned by the Anderton Company. In the foreground are the staff and the newly constructed narrow-boat *Cymric* which was built for the company itself, although they also undertook work for other owners and companies. The yard was capable of housing four boats under cover and had one slipway equipped with electric hoists for lifting boats out of the water instead of the more usual winches. Next to the boatyard is the solid warehouse built by the Anderton Company in 1890 with an unusual covered hoist on the gable end of the building. By the late nineteenth century practically all of the boatyards were in the large urban areas, such as Stoke-on-Trent. The Mersey, Weaver and Ship Canal Carrying Company however, had a boatyard at Longport and Samuel Fox had another at Westport. This is in contrast with the earlier period typified by the boatyard at Barlaston.

35 A romantic view of Longport and Burslem drawn during the 1840s. Burslem, often called the 'Mother of the Potteries', lies to the right of the tree, dominated by its clustered bottle kilns and engine chimneys. The canal did not succeed in drawing established works to new canalside locations; instead a branch canal and tramroad were opened in 1804 to link Burslem to the canal. However, a new breed of entrepreneurial potters chose to build their works adjacent to the canal and this gave life to a new community at Longport (seen to the left of the tree). There were extensive wharves at Longport which handled a considerable part of the raw materials and manufactured goods, to and from Tunstall and Burslem; including one belonging to the Hendra Company, which supplied potters' materials to most of the local master-potters.

36　The distinguished novelist H.G. Wells visited Shelton Iron-works during the 1890s and subsequently used it as the setting for his macabre story *The Cone*. From the time of his visit the appearance of the works had changed little by the early 1930s, when this photograph was taken. The locomotive is engaged in turning a bogie filled with molten slag onto one of the tips which bordered the canal. Canal water was used for cooling the blast furnaces and Wells described its condition on re-entering the canal as being: 'a tumultuous, almost boiling affluent, and steam rose up from the water in silent white wisps and streaks'. Originally, the Shelton furnaces had been situated close to Hanley and they were blown in during 1841. The furnaces were moved to the present canalside location in 1858 and remained in blast until their final closure in 1978.

37 Josiah Wedgwood, mindful of the lack of room for expansion in Burslem and the advantage of a canal-side location, bought the Ridgehouse estate in what became Etruria. In December 1767, he spent two days 'at Hetruria, in seting out the canal' and trying to persuade Hugh Henshall to alter the line of the canal so that it would run through his estate. Henshall, who Wedgwood described as an 'inflexible vandal', would not alter the line of the canal, claiming that he had to take the most direct route or Brindley would be furious. Three months later Wedgwood's problems were made worse when John Brindley and a group of other potters objected to any deviation in the proposed route that would be to his advantage. Wedgwood tackled them at a committee meeting and clearly got his way. Work started on the factory early in 1768 and it was practically completed towards the end of the same year.

38 The site chosen by Wedgwood for his Etruria factory was where the recently turnpiked Newcastle-Leek road crossed the amended line of the canal. The works became the nucleus of an industrial village which included workers' cottages and a mansion for Wedgwood himself. As Professor S. H. Beaver has demonstrated, comparatively few potters followed Wedgwood's example and moved to canal-side locations. This was due to the simple economic fact concerning the relative proportions of coal and clay used in pottery factories. At least six times as much coal as clay was required to make a given quantity of ware, so it was better to stay in the towns which were on the exposed coal measures. The Etruria works were supplied with coal from a number of sources, but chief among the suppliers were the Gilberts'

Harecastle Collieries and the Cockshead Colliery on the Caldon Canal. This photograph shows the works eleven years before they were demolished in 1968.

39 One of the greatest natural threats to canal traffic was ice, as canal companies very quickly realised. Sir Joseph Banks described an ice-breaker at work at Worsley in 1767 and clearly it was to be the inspiration for all future boats. He relates how 'a broad stemmd boat in which were 7 or 8 men who swayd her with great force as she was drawn on by the mule. The excellence of this way is not easily conceived till seen for swaying a boat in a canal so narrow a large wave runs before her which always cracks and often separates the ice before she touches it.' Here an ice-breaker is seen at work near Etruria in the winter of 1940. Teams of horses were used to haul the ice-breaker and Henry Wedgwood relates how during the 1830s up to fifteen horses were used on an ice-breaker near the Etruria factory.

40 On the same occasion that the traditional ice-breaker was at work, the maintenance crew at Etruria carried out something of an experiment. Using the diesel-powered canal tug they are seen here breaking up packed ice on the Etruria stretch of the canal. Apart from ice, delays could be caused by floods, repairs, or a shortage of water which became a very significant consideration when canals had to compete with the speed and regularity of the railways. Of all the problems caused by adverse weather conditions, the most persistent was the shortage of water. The Trent and Mersey Canal experienced a general shortage of water, but the years 1785, 1788-9, and 1791 were particularly bad. William Robinson, the principal agent, stated that in 1785 and 1795 both the canals and reservoirs had run dry, adding that even in a good year 'many boats had to navigate with half loads in the dry season'.

41

41 During the last phase of commercial activity on the canals motor boats were the most common craft and they doubtless enabled canal boating to survive until recent times. This photograph was taken in 1950 near Cliff Vale and it shows a motorised coal boat and its butty *Persia*. Much of this coal was loaded from a conveyor belt at the Sideway Loading Plant (sometimes known as Cockshute Wharf as it was adjacent to the Cockshute railway sidings). The most significant customer for slack coal at this time was Henry Seddons, the salt manufacturers at Middlewich who continued to receive their coal in this way until 1969. Henry Seddon also had boats of his own which were used mainly to convey salt from Middlewich to Anderton, where the salt was transhipped to Weaver flats. When the company disposed of their boats in 1960 they were operating four narrow boats.

42 Because of the landforms in the area of the North Staffordshire pottery towns, the canal was restricted to the valley of the Fowlea Brook. This meant that of the six towns, only Stoke actually lay on the canal. Clearly, this was a problem and a number of schemes were implemented to make communication with the canal easier. Burslem was connected to the canal by means of a branch canal opened by 1804 and a tramroad; Hanley, Fenton and Longton were all served by two tramroads. These tramroads were built by the canal company during 1803-4 with John Rennie as the engineer. The surviving section of the Lane End tramroad near Pratts Siding, shown in the photograph, was relaid with mammoth plate-rails in the late nineteenth century and remained in use well into this century.

THE CANAL, TRENTHAM.

43 The narrow boat *Ireland* belonged to the Salt Union and bore the fleet number '95'. Here she is seen approaching the canal bridge at Hem Heath (near Trentham) just prior to World War I. The small boy leading the horse adds to the charm of the scene, while the boatman appears to be reading a newspaper and ignoring the tiller. The Salt Union was founded in 1888 and it brought together sixty-four saltworks, including the one at Shirleywich, near Stafford. At this time, they also acquired the boats of existing salt proprietors and manufacturers and so assembled their large fleet of boats. *Ireland* is probably returning from Shirleywich (also alongside the Trent and Mersey Canal) when this picture was taken and she is carrying a partial load of staves for the pottery crate makers. The bridge is a good example of the type erected by the North Staffordshire Railway Company to replace the original ones.

44 A narrow boat about to leave the top lock at Meaford during the 1930s. Originally, the canal climbed to this point by means of a staircase of three locks followed by a single lock. This must have caused considerable congestion and ultimately the company decided to do something about it. The destruction of the company's records prevent the work from being precisely dated, but it was probably carried out around 1831 when they sought land nearby at Barlaston to duplicate a lock. The style of reconstruction also suggests it was part of the programme of work which Telford carried out during the same period. At Meaford, the canal was re-routed and straightened to the east of the original line which had followed the 350ft contour. Henshall's staircase locks were replaced by three new and separate locks, although the top lock was left unaltered.

45 On Meaford Canal, Stone.

46

45   The upper-most lock of the staircase was retained to serve as an overflow weir for the pound above the lock shown in this photograph. The original line of the canal can still be traced along with the remnants of the staircase locks. The channel is well worth examining as it clearly reveals the profile of the original canal — deep enough for boats only in the centre, with shallow sides to allow for the displacement of the water. In this small area it is possible to compare the construction of the early canal built in the tradition of mill leats with a stretch of canal built in the positive style typified by Telford's Shropshire Union Canal. Taken in the early 1920s this photograph shows the new stretch of canal along with two early pleasure craft. The boat nearest the camera looks very similar to the one photographed at Marbury in 1907.

46   The head offices of the Trent and Mersey Canal Company were at Stone, which also possessed an extensive boat building and repair yard which is still in use. No date is known for the docks, but the age and size of the bricks suggest they may be contemporary with the adjacent stretch of canal. The yard contains four dry docks, two built with roofs, one supported by iron pillars and the other by brick piers. One of those built originally without a roof has been given a modern covering. The docks were built just upstream from a lock and are emptied by sluices which drain the water to the next level. The photograph shows *Arabia*, owned by British Waterways Board undergoing alterations at Stone in 1955. One of the covered docks can be seen to the left of the picture. There are two substantial workshops at the yard and in 1968 the sawpits for this yard were still visible nearby.

47   This photograph shows Great Haywood Junction, where the Trent and Mersey Canal is joined by the Staffordshire and Worcestershire Canal. In the foreground of the photograph is the last bridge across the Staffordshire and Worcestershire, No 109, which carries the towpath of the Trent and Mersey. This brick roving bridge is of a particularly striking design and, to facilitate the turning of boats, unusually wide. The Act for the Staffordshire and Worcestershire Canal was passed on the same day as that for the Trent and Mersey Canal, so provision was simultaneously made for joining the Trent, Mersey and Severn rivers. James Brindley has always been credited with the surveying of the canal and his assistants with its construction, although records of his involvement are at best fragmentary. However, new evidence shows that the line was surveyed by John Gilbert, who also steered the Act through both houses of Parliament.

47

48 A photograph which captures something of the tranquil nature of the rural stretches of the canal. Here a narrow boat approaches Great Haywood in 1910. The stretch of canal between Shugborough and Stone was opened in 1771 and the next year became increasingly busy when the Staffordshire and Worcestershire Canal was completed. At nearby Wolsley Bridge, a crucial meeting was held on 30 December 1765, at which according to Josiah Wedgwood: 'There were rival schemes before the meeting'. Earl Gower made the most significant speach and as a result, Brindley's submission was taken up with few reservations. The meeting approved the idea of forming a junction with the projected Bridgewater Canal to Runcorn, the exact route having been surveyed by Hugh Henshall in the months prior to the meeting. The meeting closed with an expressed determination to seek parliamentary powers.

49 Most of the bridges built on the Trent and Mersey Canal and its branches were of a standard design, identical with this bridge at Little Haywood which was strengthened in October 1973. Each stretch of canal cut across farms and estates, as well as roads; and since access had to be maintained, a large number of bridges were built. They are clearly inspired by the bridges on the Bridgewater Canal with a 'hump-backed' style for the shorter the approach, the less expensive they were to build. The shape of the arch was achieved by laying the bricks over a wooden frame, called the centring. These bridges have proved to be very durable and difficult to demolish.

49

50 The canal agent's house at Rugeley Wharf in the period just prior to World War I. During this period H.C. James represented the North Staffordshire Railway and Canal Company, having been transferred to Rugeley in 1904. He had started work for the company at the Etruria Check Office, before being sent to Kings Lock, Middlewich, in 1893, where he was responsible for the wharves in that area. Agents held very responsible positions controlling the lock-keepers, wharfingers, and carrying staff in the days when the canal company ran its own boats, the engineer, the masons, carpenters and other craftsmen, the lengthsman and labourers who worked along the banks, and the reservoir-keepers. Like many canal staff, H.C. James had well established family links with the canal including a brother-in-law who was canal agent at the Etruria Check Office in 1892.

50

51 H.C. James was also a keen amateur photographer and he took this picture of the *Dragon Fly* at Rugeley Wharf, in 1910. The boat belonged to Henry Rodolph de Salis, a director of Fellows, Morton and Clayton, canal carriers chiefly on the Birmingham to London routes, and a member of a family who had been associated with canals since the eighteenth century. From 1887 to 1901, de Salis travelled in excess of 14,000 miles over English and Welsh waterways, a feat which is certain to remain unparalleled. His journeying resulted in the publication of *Bradshaw's Canals and Navigable Rivers of England and Wales*, in 1904.

51

52 This is another photograph taken by H. C. James on 30 May 1924, shortly after the Brereton Colliery basin had closed. Coal was brought to this basin from the Brereton Colliery by a tram-road constructed by Lord Shrewsbury in 1815-16. It crossed the main Rugeley to Lichfield road near Brereton church, but after an accident the crossing was replaced by a tunnel which still survives as a subway. In the 1880s horse haulage was withdrawn and edge-rails laid with an engine which continued to haul the waggons until the line closed. At the wharf the loads were checked and tipped into canal boats, then the empty waggons were made up into trains for the return journey. Stacked sleepers and sleeper impressions can be seen in this photograph showing that the tramway had been dismantled by this date.

53 Armitage Tunnel, shown here in 1910, has the distinction of being the first British canal

tunnel to be built with a towpath through it. Originally, it was intended to carve a tunnel nearly 200yd long, but unstable rock reduced its length to 130yd. Like the 500yd section in the middle of the first Harecastle Tunnel, the Armitage Tunnel was not lined with brickwork.

54   Both Earl Gower and Thomas Gilbert objected to the mention of 'the amusements of a Gondola' in Bentley's pamphlet, arguing that such a consideration was 'trifleing'. Yet by 1780, the canal company possessed a 'committee boat' which was used mainly for tours of inspection, although it also seems to have been used for pleasure trips. In the same year, committeemen Josiah Wedgwood and Edward Sneyd used the boat to take their families along the Caldon Canal to visit Thomas Gilbert at Cotton Hall. The Directors of the North Staffordshire Railway Company had their own inspection launch built during the 1860s. She was known as the *Dolly Varden* after the character in Charles Dickens' *Barnaby Rudge* and the photograph shows her in her rebuilt form. When the

first sod of the Manifold Light Railway was turned in 1899, this launch was used to convey company dignitaries to Froghall Wharf, before being taken up the incline to the ceremony.

55   The horse-drawn narrow boat *Ethel* approaching Fradley Junction in 1939 with a load of barrels. Here the Coventry Canal, to the right of the photograph, joins the Trent and Mersey Canal. The former was opened through to Coventry in 1790, after years of dispute between the canal companies, and

it filled an important gap in the cross-country canal routes. The Swan Inn at Fradley Junction is a splendid example of a boatman's inn, built of red brick in the Georgian style of architecture. The inn is sandwiched between a cottage, originally built for one of the company's agents, and stables, so that the needs of men and horses could have been met in this once isolated spot. There is also a maintenance yard nearby, serving the length of the canal from Burton to Trentham, which it is believed was established in 1872.

56

57

56 At Monks Bridge, between Stretton and Eggington, the canal is carried across the meadows of the Dove valley on an embankment 13ft high and over the main stream of the River Dove by an aqueduct. By later standards this is a rather ordinary structure but at the time of its construction it was a major achievement. The aqueduct is made up of twelve arches, although as the photograph shows, only half of that number are normally required to accommodate the river. One explanation of this is that Brindley built the aqueduct in two halves, diverting the river away from the working area until half the aqueduct had been completed and then again diverting the river to build the second half. A more likely explanation is that Brindley was making a generous allowance for the accommodation of flood waters, the scale of which he could not accurately forecast.

57 *Buffalo,* another of the motor boats owned by Fellows, Morton and Clayton, seen between Stenson and Barrow-on-Trent in the early 1940s. Commissioned in January 1924, this was an iron composite boat built at Northwich by W. J. Yarwood & Sons Ltd. Boats belonging to Fellows, Morton and Clayton were among the last commercial craft seen on the eastern section of the Trent and Mersey. They worked in pairs, a steamer or motor boat towing a butty boat. The company carried every conceivable type of cargo, including coal which represented the bulk of their more localised loads. Another important cargo they carried was sugar from London and Liverpool. On 1 January 1948 most of the canals were nationalised and this seems to have adversely affected the firm. Subsequently they made their first trading loss ever and they sold out to the British Transport Commission in 1949.

58 The junction with the Derby canal at Swarkestone in 1960. James Brindley had surveyed a proposed branch, to Chesterfield via Derby, as early as 1771 but it was another twenty-one years before the Derby Canal Company came into being. The canal was eventually extended eastwards to the Erewash Canal, and northwards to the Little Eaton tramroad which served the collieries around Denby. The Derby Canal Company operated an interesting weekly return service from Swarkestone to Derby: 'A Market Boat, decked over, with seats, and a fireplace, for the accommodation of Passengers'. There was a toll-house at Swarkestone junction which now serves as the headquarters of the Swarkestone Boat Club, formed in 1951. By this time, the Derby Canal was already derelict although it was not officially closed until 1964. The house-boat shown in the photograph is a converted barge.

59 Swarkestone lock and the lock keeper's cottage as they were in 1960. This lock stands on the broad eastern section of the canal between Derwent Mouth and Horninglow Wharf at Burton-on-Trent which was designed to accommodate river barges of 40 tons. In this section the canal was built 31ft wide at the top, 18ft wide at the bottom, and 5½ft deep, the locks being 14ft wide. This compares with the narrow middle section, where the canal was 29ft wide at the top, 16ft wide at the bottom, and 4½ft deep; the locks being 7ft wide and 75ft long. The northern section from Middlewich to Preston Brook was also built to the wider gauge to accommodate the Duke of Bridgewater's barges. There was an abortive proposal in the 1890s to widen and straighten the canal from Stoke to Preston Brook to take barges of up to 80 tons.

60 Shardlow is a real gem because it is one of only two canal towns in Britain which survive in something like their original state. This little port is made up of an irregular mixture of warehouses, public houses and houses, but its original purpose still remains very obvious. Before the coming of the Trent and Mersey Canal, Shardlow was a very small settlement, but it soon became clear that a new inland port would be needed near to the junction of the canal and the River Trent, which would handle the interchange of goods between canal and river craft. Although it is a mile from this point, Shardlow was the obvious site as it stood on the main Derby to Loughborough road and this ensured good road access. This view, taken in 1948, shows the former brewery and maltings on the left, since demolished; and one of the larger warehouses.

61 Repairs being carried out during 1941 to Shardlow Lock. By the lock stands the former Canal Tavern, a late nineteenth-century public house standing on the site of the only river warehouse existing at the time of Shardlow's development as a canal port. This public house has been immortalised by an affectionate description in L. T. C. Rolt's *Narrow Boat*. When Tom and Angela Rolt called, they found that the landlord was a blacksmith by day, and an amateur musician by night who would 'thump out' well loved songs on an aged piano. Understandably, Shardlow possessed a considerable number of public houses and three still survive. The oldest is The Navigation, at the top of Wilne Lane, which was built when Shardlow was a minor river port. The New Inn is the oldest of the canal era public houses; and The Malt Shovel occupies a building dating from 1799, although it was originally a private dwelling.

59

62 All canal companies were determined to facilitate the collection of tolls, hence the expense they incurred in erecting mile-posts, and few of these mile-posts can be as elegant as those erected by the Trent and Mersey Canal Company between 1819-20. These are of cast-iron indicating the distances between Preston Brook and Shardlow; or in the case of the Caldon and Uttoxeter branches between Etruria and Uttoxeter. This mile-post is the zero one at Shardlow where it will be found next to the Lady in Grey restaurant. All the mile-posts came from the foundry of Rangeley and Dixon, which stood in Lichfield Road, Stone, not far from the company's head office. John Rangeley was an inventor from Yorkshire and the main production of the foundry took the form of 'Patent Roller Pumps'. The same style of mile-posts were also supplied to local turnpike trusts.

63 This is how the so-called Shardlow Mill looked in 1948. It had been built in 1792 by the canal company as a warehouse, and originally the boats passed under the arches to unload, thus being protected from inclement weather. Later the warehouse was converted into a corn mill and it is still used for that purpose. The construction of warehouses at Shardlow was a gradual process and the reason is revealed in the canal company's report for 1787. Announcing a profit of £31,239 for the previous year, Thomas Sparrow points out that the company could not undertake the 'many things necessary to its support and accomodation' as the money was required to pay dividends. The report also reveals that an increase in trade had made the expansion and erection of certain wharves and warehouses absolutely necessary. In the same year the company had to spend a massive £4,832 on repairs to Bagnall Reservoir.

64 The oldest dated warehouse at Shardlow is this three-storeyed building, built in 1780 by the canal company. An old photograph shows that until early in the present century it bore hoardings proclaiming: NAVIGATION FROM THE TRENT TO THE MERSEY. Considering this and its prominent position, the building was clearly something of a prestige project which was intended to say something about the status and aspirations of the company. As it originally housed a clock, it was known to boatmen as the clock warehouse, and like the company's other warehouse it also straddled a canal arm. The photograph shows the warehouse as it was in 1948, when it was in use as a corn mill. In 1976, a hire boat firm bought the old warehouse and the nearby salt warehouse; the overgrown frontage basin has been cleared and dredged, and the warehouse has been restored in a very sympathetic way.

65 The motor boat *Rover* and butty *Grace*, two boats owned by Fellows, Morton and Clayton, seen breasted up at Shardlow during World War II. *Rover* was a wooden boat launched at Fellows, Morton and Clayton's Uxbridge boatyard in 1919. She was damaged when the Company's Fazeley Street depot was bombed during World War II and was subsequently sold off to Ernest Thomas of Walsall. The building in the background was at this time a fertiliser warehouse, but it is probably the earliest of the port buildings at Shardlow, having originally been used as a salt warehouse. The early pleasure craft may have been constructed at Dobson's old established boatyard which carries on the long tradition of boatbuilding in Shardlow. Trent barges were built in Shardlow before 1800 by Benjamin Clifford and the Gainsborough Boat Company, and Hugh Henshall and Company were also building boats here.

63

64

65

Newcastle Canal & Gresley's Canal

66 The junction of the Trent and Mersey Canal and the Newcastle-under-Lyme Canal at Stoke as it was in August 1971. This was the last remnant of the Newcastle Canal and was being used at this time as moorings for Stoke Boat Club whose headquarters were in the old warehouse seen on the right of this photograph. The unusually shaped bridge carried the towpath of the Trent and Mersey Canal over the Newcastle Canal. A branch to Newcastle had been suggested when the Trent and Mersey Canal was being promoted, but it was not considered a priority and resources were concentrated on the main line. It took the creation of the Newcastle-under-Lyme Canal Company in 1795 to get the scheme off the ground and to obtain the necessary parliamentary powers. By this time Sir Nigel Gresley had built his canal and cornered the coal trade in Newcastle.

67 This photograph is taken from a cine-film made at the Spode works before World War II. It shows a horse pulling a waggon along the internal tramroad system that connected various parts of the factory to the wharf on the banks of the Newcastle Canal. Clearly a very efficient system in its day, it emphasises the advantages that potters could draw from canalside locations. Josiah Spode I had already established his works at Stoke and he understandably made no objection to the construction of the canal which ran between his works and those of Thomas Wolfe. Despite the name of the canal it is ironical to think that the pottery manufacturers of London Road, Stoke drew more benefit from the canal than did the people of Newcastle, for whose service it had been promoted.

68

THE CANAL, BOOTHEN, STOKE-ON-TRENT.

68 The Newcastle Canal was only four miles in length and did not take long to complete. It had reached Hanford by 1796 and it was described as 'newly completed' in 1797. This print shows Church Street, Stoke in 1818 at the point where the canal emerged from a tunnel under the road. The Big Pottery Works is on the left and the Bridge Bank Pottery on the right; at this time both were owned by William Adams whose name appears on the side of the narrow boat. Both works had originally been owned and operated by Thomas Wolfe, who erected a steam engine in one of them and had its water supply safe-guarded by a clause in the canal Act. The interesting building which extends over the canal may have been for loading under cover, but there was also a branch extending into the Bridge Bank Pottery.

69 Taken about 1910, this photograph shows the Newcastle canal by Boothen School, Stoke. The whole of this section has now been filled in and planted as ornamental gardens, so it is difficult to envisage it as once being a canal. A granite obelisk survives by the road recalling a tragic incident in 1894, when a young tram conductor drowned in the canal in an attempt to save the life of a child. A report of 1845 records that as there were no public baths 'every facility exists for public bathing in the canal'. This practice was banned by a bye-law of the Trent and Mersey Canal Company, but the New-castle Canal Company seemed to have allowed it. The wisdom of the bathers must be doubted as another contemporary report described the canal as 'stagnant' and a 'health hazard'. In 1828 a nude bather wandered too far from the Newcastle Junction Canal and offended some prominent citizens.

70 The only surviving bridge on the Newcastle Canal stands at Oakhill and this photograph shows it as it was in August 1971. Beyond the bridge is a coalyard which survived the abandonment of the canal and in the foreground is a small building erected as a joinery workshop. An important early traffic on the canal was lime and the terminal basin at Brook Lane, Newcastle was the site of two limekilns which did a brisk trade and yielded a yearly income of £63 to the Newcastle Canal Company. The canal was a totally unprofitable venture for the shareholders who did not receive a dividend until 1840. The problem was that the lucrative coal trade was confined to Gresley's Canal and the Newcastle Junction Canal, which were never connected to the Newcastle Canal.

71 The Newcastle-under-Lyme Canal survived for some years as an independent company but it was finally acquired by the North Staffordshire Railway Company in 1863. The canal remained in use throughout the remainder of the century although the inward trade to Newcastle was insignificant. This photograph shows the canal to the north of Clayton Lane Bridge in 1921, by which time the stretch of the canal between Trent Vale and Newcastle had been abandoned. The remainder of the canal had been filled in as far as Church Street, Stoke by 1938.

72 No contemporary photographs are available of the terminal wharf in Brook Lane, Newcastle, where the canal was joined by a branch railway to Silverdale, built in 1853. This view (dating from 1910) shows the canal near to the former Stoke Workhouse, which stood opposite Newcastle Corporation's sewage works. The sewage superintendent's house can be seen to the right of the bridge which gave access to the works.

73 A view of Holditch Bridge on the then derelict Gresley's Canal as it appeared on the eve of World War I. The canal was built under powers granted in an Act of 1775 by Sir Nigel Gresley and his son Sir Nigel Bowyer Gresley, for the purpose of conveying coal from their collieries to Newcastle-under-Lyme. This Act bound the Gresley's for twenty-one years to supply coal at their Newcastle Wharf at the fixed price of 5s per ton; and at 5s 6d for the ensuing twenty-one years. Sir Nigel Gresley died in 1787 and his son in 1808, both having been for some years hamstrung by the restrictive clauses in the Act which had greatly benefitted the town. Because of 'the great riots, injuries and disturbances' that had taken place at the coal wharf over deliveries of coal new arrangements were made in 1812 which allowed increases in the price of coal.

74 Apedale Ironworks as they appeared shortly before their demolition in the 1930s. The outline of the works is reflected in a section of Gresley's Canal which had survived as a pond serving the blast engine at the works. The first furnaces on the site had been put into blast in 1784 by Abraham Parker, who belonged to a famous Black Country family of ironmasters. Then the use of the canal was limited to conveying raw materials to the works and taking finished iron to the turnpike road, where it ran parallel with the canal at Dimsdale. The lack of a direct link with the national canal network must have been a serious handicap to the works. By 1795 'Parker and Company of Newcastle' were operating no less than eight narrow boats on the Trent and Mersey Canal; and presumably like the Silverdale Iron Company, they conveyed their goods to Stoke Wharf by waggon.

HOLDITCH BRIDGE, CHESTERTON, STAFFS.

73

74

75 Burley Bridge on Gresley's Canal as it was about 1910. The bridge is of an unusual design, one arch accommodating the channel of the canal and the other the towpath. It was not an original bridge (which copied the design favoured by the Trent and Mersey Canal Company) and it probably dates from the first half of the nineteenth century. When the photograph was taken this stretch of canal also formed part of the Apedale engine pond hence the good standard of maintenance. The terminal basin of the canal lay beyond the bridge and it served the nearby shafts which were connected by tramroads. By 1833, one of these pits included

BURLEY BRIDGE CHESTERTON

workings 2,520ft deep, comprising a 720ft shaft and an inclined plane (worked by a sub-terranean steam engine) to the lowest level. At this time it was the deepest mine in Britain.

76

76 This is an extremely rare photograph of one of the tramroads in the Apedale Valley which had once served Gresley's Canal. The short plate rails and primative points system can be clearly seen at the base of the double tracked incline which led to the nearby pit-head. This carefully posed composition was taken in 1895 but it shows a tramroad design that was already one hundred years old at that time. Following the failure of the Commercial Canal scheme of 1795, which would have incorporated Gresley's Canal in its line, an ambitious tramroad scheme was proposed to join Gresley's Canal to the Chester Canal at Nantwich. The scheme was launched in 1805 and branches were envisaged to the Newcastle-under-Lyme Canal and to Market Drayton. Such an ambitious railway system could have provided valuable outlets for the local collieries as well as directing a lively trade to the moribund Chester Canal, but in the end the scheme proved abortive.

The Caldon Canal

77 The 17-mile long Caldon Canal leaves the summit level of the Trent and Mersey at Etruria. Shortly afterwards it reaches the Bedford Street Locks which are the only surviving examples of staircase locks in North Staffordshire. This photograph shows the entrance to one of the locks and a bridge in 1940. The bridge had been hit by a bomb, intended for the nearby Shelton Steel Works and had to be demolished. The idea for the Caldon Canal was first mooted in 1772 and during the next year a plan was prepared which proposed to use inclined planes instead of locks. The chief traffic was to be in limestone from the Cauldon Low quarries with some coal from the Cheadle Coalfield. The company were just as interested in bringing down additional water to the summit level of the main canal, as they were in building a navigable canal.

78

79

78 The Etruria Lock and check office on the Caldon Canal in 1892, showing the roof which once covered the lock. The carefully posed group includes a number of canal officials. The bearded gentleman is Mr Corbishley, the canal engineer; next to him is Richard Leese, canal agent at Etruria; and on his right is H. C. James who was working in the check office at this time but eventually became canal agent at Rugeley. By his side is Mrs James, who was the sister of Mrs Rosella Leese who is seen holding her niece, Lilian James, aged one. The boat's crew have also been included and their dress is fairly typical of the period, especially the corduroy trousers.

79 Potters' millers, on the Caldon Canal at Etruria Vale, in 1948. The narrow boat is *Durban* which belonged to George Mellor and Company, of Etruria Vale Mill, who dealt in coal and potters' materials. They acquired the boat in 1945 and used it mainly to bring coal from Sideway loading plant, a function which it was still fulfilling in 1953. Plans are well advanced for establishing a waterways museum on this site which incorporates many significant buildings. This will also involve the preservation of a beam engine at Shirley's Etruscan bone mill. This steam engine dates back to 1830 and is believed to have been built by local engineers John and Thomas Sherratt. It is of particular interest as it is said to have been built for a paddle steamer, and their father, William Sherratt, installed an engine in an early steam craft for the Duke of Bridgewater.

80 Johnson Brothers, part of the earthenware division of the Wedgwood group, use three specially built narrow boats to carry finished ware between the Hanley factories and their packing house at Milton, conveniently connected by the Caldon Canal. Here ware is being loaded aboard the *Milton Queen* at Eastwood, Hanley in 1974. The *Milton Maid* was introduced in 1967 and six years later the *Milton Queen* was launched to increase their effective use of the canal. The boats are about 60ft long and 7ft wide and can carry 20 tons of ware. Both boats were designed by Geoffrey Bird, Johnson Brothers former engineering executive and were built in a disused warehouse at one of the Johnson factories.

81

82

81 The *Milton Queen* heading for Milton with a load of ware. The boats actually cost much less than one of the specially designed lorry trailers, which can carry only a third of the cargo of one of the boats. Transporting ware over the short distance by canal reduces costs by nearly 50 per cent compared with the use of lorries, and the elimination of road hazards cuts the number of breakages by over two-thirds. *Milton Princess* is the third boat to be operated by the company, who had it specially built by M. E. Braine, boatbuilders at Norton Cane Docks, Pelsall, near Walsall. This boat can carry about forty cages of ware or 3,000 pieces on an average trip, taking one hour for the journey to Milton. A hydraulic lift system on board rises to dock level and two hinged ramps make loading easy.

82 The pioneer boat built by Johnson Brothers, the *Milton Maid* has turned turtle three times during its working life. Each time some £3,000 worth of ware, not to mention the boatman, has been tipped into the Caldon Canal, although losses have never exceeded £200. On 5 May 1975 this catamaran-style boat overturned near Birches Head Road and deposited £5,000 worth of export orders into the canal. As the photograph shows, about a dozen men were rushed to the scene to recover the ware from the canal bottom. Some of the men recovering the ware were provided with wet suits and a winch to recover the steel cages. These incidents are exceptions and the boats have proved to be a tremendous success and hopefully an inspiration to other manufacturers. If fuel costs continue to rise, the Wedgwood group may extend the use of the boats to the Trent and Mersey Canal itself.

83 An aerial oblique view of Eagle Pottery, Hanley taken during the 1920s. These works represent a classical example of a canalside location, although the site had originally been occupied by a foundry. The main wharf area can be seen alongside the canal where there is a gap in the frontage, and from here materials were drawn up into the factory by means of a small inclined tramway. The factory is owned by J. and G. Meakin, who also had their own boats which ran to and from the docks at Weston Point and Runcorn, carrying earthenware down and potters' material back. The company operated three horse-drawn narrow boats: *Cuba, Darlaston* and *Westwood* which handled most of their export traffic until 1932. In 1944, they bought a new motor-powered boat called *Alice* which operated on the same route until the company ceased to use the canal in 1953.

83

84 The narrow boat *Havelock* rising in one of the locks at Stockton Brook in 1939. At this time the boat had been owned by Thomas Bolton and Sons for two years, and they used it to carry coal slack to their Froghall works and general cargoes on the Trent and Mersey Canal. Boltons bought the boat from Arthur Johnson, a 'number one' (owner-boatman) of Etruria and they operated it until 1953 when it was sold. The roses and castles painted on the cabin doors are typical of those once seen on the Trent and Mersey Canal and are thought to be the work of a local painter, William Hodgson. He is considered to have been one of the greatest of the boat painters, and his work is best known from the period when he worked for the Anderton Company at their Middleport boatyard.

85 Volunteers working on the back-breaking and often extremely unpleasant task of cleaning out one of the Stockton Brook locks. This is only one of the seventeen locks on the Caldon Canal, most of which have had to be similarly treated. Indeed the canal would certainly have been lost if it was not for the Caldon Canal Society, who organised an ambitious programme of work. This involved many thousands of man hours in addition to an actual cost saving of £10,000 during the main restoration programme. However, the Society's main achievement was to interest the two local authorities, Stoke-on-Trent City Council and Staffordshire County Council in the potential of the canal. To the numerous volunteers (many of whom were not members of the Society) it seemed grossly inappropriate that the local authority should claim back the estimated cost of voluntary labour from the Waterways Board.

86 John Rennie had disagreed with Hugh Henshall that a three-rise staircase lock should be built at Hazelhurst, as part of the realignment caused by the construction of the Leek Canal. However, his advice was ignored and the congestion he feared became a feature of working through these locks. The situation was so bad that in 1841-2, the canal company decided to make radical changes. The three separate 'New Hazelhurst Locks' were built (with distinctive side pounds), and the Caldon Canal was diverted northwards to part of its original course. But as it was now obstructed by the embanked Leek Canal, Hazelhurst aqueduct had to be built, allowing the main canal to pass underneath it. At this time, a large rendered lock-keeper's cottage was built by the 'New Locks', its bay window ensuring a good view up and down the canal.

87, 88 and **89**   Unlike some railway companies, the North Staffordshire Railway Company never deliberately set out to run down the canals which it owned, but instead it tried to operate them as profit making concerns. This sometimes involved the use of railway/canal interchange facilities and of these the most intriguing was the so called 'Endon tip'. During World War I there was an insatiable demand for limestone, so much so that handling facilities at Froghall Wharf became strained to the limit. A novel solution was to bring limestone down the standard gauge line to Leekbrook Junction, then down the Leek and Bucknall branch to Endon where it could be transhipped to waiting narrow boats. In 1917 a tippling machine was built in the railway workshops at Stoke and transported to a site at Endon Basin, where the railway and the Caldon Canal ran close to one another. The tippling machine was designed by J. H. Coleman and this series of photographs show it undergoing commissioning trials in the same year. Waggons of limestone were clamped to the 'tip' and the whole thing gradually tilted to allow a carefully regulated flow of limestone to fall into the waiting narrow boat. Tradition has it that on the first occasion the flow was too sudden and the narrow boat sank, but its operation was soon perfected and it was still working in 1928. Coleman later went to the Derby locomotive works where he worked as a designer with Stanier. Of him it has been said that he was 'able to hit the target of practical and effective design in nearly everything he undertook'.

90 The last boat to be engaged regularly in the coal trade on the Caldon Canal belonged to George Tomkinson of Stockton Brook. He loaded coal slack at Endon Wharf which he took along the canal to Cheddleton Paper Mills until 1951. At Cheddleton he off-loaded onto a conveyor belt, while his famed skewbald pony contentedly ate his oats. A number of enthusiasts period-ically attempt to re-establish the old trade in coal, and in April 1976 two of them appeared on the Caldon Canal. Colin and Pat Walker loaded sixteen tons of coal at Penkridge and brought it up the canal system to Cheddle-ton. The photograph shows their 72ft narrow boat at Denford on its return journey, after what proved to be a disappointing response.

91 A narrow boat loaded with sacks full of potters' materials, overhauling an empty boat, to the north of Cheddleton during the early years of this century. Potters' materials to and from the mills at Bucknall, Cheddleton and Consall Forge were an important traffic on the Caldon Canal. Narrow boats brought the stones, flints and coal to the mills and returned with ground flint to The Potteries. The flints came from South-East England, East Anglia and France by ship to Runcorn, thence by narrow boat via the Bridgewater Canal and Trent and Mersey Canal. There was also a lively trade in coal on the Caldon Canal and Uttoxeter Canal and supplies from the Kidsgrove collieries were delivered to both Froghall and Uttoxeter before 1820. Other major suppliers, whose boats were commonly seen along the two branch canals, included Sparrow and Hales who operated the highly successful Cockshead Colliery at Norton.

92 According to John Farey: 'until about the year 1785, men were employed in large gangs, to drag the boats' on the Trent and Mersey Canal; although by 1808 horses were 'universally used for towing'. This is not to say that horses or other animals were not used, as indeed in 1774 the company introduced a by-law aimed at boatmen who allowed horses 'to go loose on towpaths'. And by 1802, further powers were acquired to deal with boatmen who fed their horses on 'corn or grass growing on lands contiguous to the Navigation'. A good horse could pull a boat for eighteen hours, although it would need regular feeds throughout the day and a good grooming at night. This photograph shows a boatman and his apparently contented horse at Cheddleton in 1900. The boat belonged to Brunner-Mond and was carrying a full load of limestone.

93 The Cheddleton Flint Mill used the River Churnet to power its two undershot waterwheels and the Caldon Canal for transport. The importance of the canal to the mill is stressed by a fascinating internal tramroad system, which dates from about 1815 when the mill was worked by John Leigh. The mill has been restored as a working example of the traditional method of producing calcined and ground flint for the pottery industry.

94 The Cheddleton Flint Mill was one of three businesses within a small industrial complex: the others being an ale and porter brewery, and a silk mill. This photograph shows the silk mill in 1900, as well as the wharf area at Cheddleton. A boat carrying coal can be seen across the mouth of the bridge, having discharged at least one wheel-barrow full of her load. To the right one of the Brunner-Mond boats is tied up, while on the opposite bank an interesting example of an ice-breaker is moored by the former boatyard.

93

94

95

96

95 A photograph taken in the same period as the previous one, but showing Cheddleton Wharf in the icy grip of winter. Another fully loaded Brunner-Mond boat is tied up, and the boatman may even be returning from a local inn, as this was a favourite stopping place. Limestone was being brought down to Cheddleton from Cauldon Low right from the earliest days of the canal, for it was here that enormous limekilns were erected in 1778 by the Cheddleton Lime Company. The partners included John Gilbert and his son John, as well as several others who worked quarries at Cauldon Low. They obtained coal from the nearby Shafferlong Coalfield, and the smoking kilns caused so much nuisance to the local people that yearly damages had to be paid. The company ceased operations in 1834 and there is no evidence that the kilns were ever used again, although they still survive. The building with the ventilator on the roof is the former Cheddleton Brewery, while to its left is the old silk mill.

97 Cheddleton top lock in 1974, one of the two lock chambers that had to be completely rebuilt by British Waterways Board workmen during the restoration of the canal. In addition to dredging work, the Board's workmen replaced nine sets of top and bottom lock gates and carried out remedial work to locks, by-weirs and other associated structures. Some of the locks were even equipped with the latest hydraulic paddle gear. It was a very different scene from the pre-restoration era, when the Waterways Board were unable to put money into work on the canal other than that required for maintenance to the standard of a waterway channel. In the background of the photograph, the chimneys of Brittains Ltd paper-making works can be seen. The existing factory is modern but paper has been produced on the site since 1797, when William Adams set up a factory here, but production ceased at Cheddleton in 1979.

96 The bottom lock at Cheddleton about 1972 showing the derelict state of the Caldon Canal before its restoration. The sluices for the ground paddles are clearly seen.

98 The British Waterways Board, in conjunction with Staffordshire County Council, Stoke-on-Trent City Council and the Caldon Canal Society, carried out restoration work on the Caldon Canal over two and a half years. On 28 September 1974 the widow of the former Chairman of the Staffordshire County Council, Mrs G. Oxford, and the Lord Mayor of Stoke-on-Trent, in the presence of the Chairman of the British Waterways Board, Sir Frank Price, jointly declared the Canal to be open once again to navigation. After cutting the tape and unveiling a commemorative plaque at Cheddleton Top Lock, the official party and guests embarked on a 'flotilla' of boats and cruised to Consall Forge for a buffet lunch. There was a slight touch of irony about the re-opening of the Caldon Canal as it had never been formally opened at Christmas 1778, but to many boating enthusiasts it was the realisation of a dream.

99 The narrow boat *Beatrice* seen approaching Woods Lock, to the south of Cheddleton, in 1915. At this time, the boat was owned by Brunner-Mond, who used it to transport broken limestone from Froghall Wharf to their Cheshire works. Brunner-Mond (later the chemical division of Imperial Chemical Industries) operated alkali works at Northwich; and they were among the most important customers for Cauldon limestone between the 1880s and 1920. The company operated a fleet of about ten narrow boats in this traffic, and they appear on many photographs of the canal during this period. During World War I they gradually sought supplies elsewhere, so *Beatrice* was sold to Thomas Bolton and Sons in 1916.

100 One of the best known boats on the Caldon Canal during the last forty years of its commercial life was *Perpetual*, owned by William Podmore and Sons of Consall Mills. The boat was first registered to the Anderton Company and named *Brussels* being purchased by William Podmore in October 1915. It was horse-drawn and operated mainly between Consall Mills, and the company's head office and Caledonian Mills, at Shelton which also lay on the Caldon Canal. Consall Mills chiefly produced ground Cornish stone and calcined flint and this was conveyed to Shelton in both dry and slop conditions. Close to Consall Mills, William Podmore also worked Crowgutter Mill where flint was ground and pumped into boats in a slop condition, loading only taking some twenty minutes. The boats engaged in this traffic were known locally as 'Buttermilk Boats' and included one owned by a Mr Jackson.

101 The original mile-posts erected by the canal company were far more fundamental in their design and execution, than the elegant Rangeley and Dixon mile-posts which were erected in the period 1819-20. This sandstone mile-post was uncovered near Consall Forge where it had gradually been buried by soil creep. It dates from shortly after the opening of the Caldon Canal in 1778 and it is the only one to survive in something like its original condition. The '3' records the distance in miles to Froghall Wharf (the Uttoxeter Canal did not open until 1811) and the '14' the distance to Etruria. The later mile-post, in the background, bears the lettering 'Etruria 14 Miles', and 'Uttoxeter 16 Miles'. The basic idea behind each of the designs is the same, although the distance to Etruria is shown on different faces of each of the mile-posts.

102 The joys of travelling leisurely through a sylvan glade. A Sunday outing, in the years before the outbreak of World War I, in the boat *Farmers Friend* which belonged to Bowers and Thorley, lime burners at Froghall Wharf. Francis Hordern is at the tiller as the boat passes through Consall Forge. Such trips were especially popular during the Whitsuntide and August holidays. The potters of Stoke-on-Trent patronised excursions on ornate canal boats from Etruria and Stoke to Trentham and sometimes beyond to Barlaston. The boats were divested of their trade appointments, cleaned up and painted, provided with seats and their brasswork polished. On these occasions they carried considerable numbers of people at the horse's pace the six miles to Trentham. Men usually had to stand the whole way, but they did it cheerfully, thankful for the opportunity of spending a few hours in the countryside.

103 One of the small number of narrow boats that boated lime-stone to South Staffordshire, seen approaching Consall Forge in the early years of this century. The section of the canal between here and Oakmeadowford Lock uses the bed of the River Churnet, which falls over a weir to the right of the footbridge.

104 *Shannon*, laden with lime-stone, passing from the Canal into the River Churnet at Consall Forge early this century. The flood gates protect the canal when the river is in flood. The building framed by the arch of the bridge was associated with the adjacent battery of four massive limekilns. Limestone was landed here and burnt before being transported towards Longton by a tramroad, begun in 1815. This early railway was worked by the North Stafford Railway Company between 1815 and 1832, and was part of a far more ambitious scheme, including an extension of the tramroad up the Combes Valley to the Mixon Hay limestone quarries. The railway company clearly intended to rival the Cauldon Low quarries, but they failed because of insufficient capital.

102

CONSALL, CHURNET VALLEY

105

106

105 At Consall the Churnet Valley is so narrow that when the railway was built in order to accommodate the river, canal and railway the canal was restricted in width and the platform and waiting room of the small station were centilevered over the canal.

106 The narrow boat *Dora*, belonging to Price and Son of Brierley Hill on the Dudley Canal, about 1900. *Dora* is seen here between Podmore's Flint Mill and Consall Forge with a cargo of limestone. In the background is a maintenance boat, probably a spoon dredger.

107 *Dora* again at Consall Forge, probably on the same trip. This picture clearly shows the decoration on the helm, the special rope work and swan's neck. This is a typical Midlands narrow boat, with a cratch at the fore end, although the round castle painting on the cabin door is unusual — they were more often square.

108

109

108 A delightful composition showing a narrow boat being towed back towards the winding hole at Consall Forge, about 1900. The boat has just been unloaded at the mill's wharf, which was equipped with its own crane and can be seen beyond the bridge. Consall Forge was an important ironworking centre until the mid-eighteenth century, with a forge and slitting mill. The flint mill buildings were erected in 1778 on the site of the forge, the old buildings either being demolished or converted. The mill was first operated by William Bill, Thomas Griffin and Francis Leigh. The first two were significant shareholders in the canal company, and clearly aware of the possibilities presented by the Caldon Canal. These works and another nearby, were extended by John Leigh and by 1841 they were producing 350 tubs of slop per week. Since 1918 the mills have been owned and worked by Podmore and Sons.

109 The modern means of dredging canals is illustrated in this photograph, taken between Consall Mills and Froghall in June 1974. Preserving a good depth of water and so preventing boats grounding on the bottom has always been one of the most important tasks of canal maintenance. Originally, the Trent and Mersey Canal Company employed spoon dredgers, but when the North Staffordshire Railway Company took the canal over they purchased a steam-powered grab which was at work during the 1890s. During the restoration of the Caldon Canal this land-based drag-line crane was used to remove 68,000 tonnes of silt and debris. The operator has to be particularly skilful so as not to disturb the lining of 'puddle clay'. The boat to the left of the group is a typical work flat capable of carrying several tons of silt or 'puddle clay' for bank repairs, or other materials needed for particular jobs.

110 Thomas Bolton and Sons Ltd, now part of British Insulated Callenders Cables Ltd, is the sole survivor today of the north Staffordshire copper industry. At Froghall their large copper works has spread across the valley, although it is still possible to see Alfred Sohier Bolton's first buildings, erected from 1890. Here and at their Oakamoor works, copper wire was produced with a higher and more uniform conductivity than had been previously available. Thomas Bolton, grandson of the original Thomas, was managing director of the firm by 1908; and it was he who was responsible for the gradual acquisition of the firm's narrow boats which were used to bring coal slack to the works for use in the steam generating plant. Here one of the firm's boats is seen being towed back to the winding hole after unloading outside the steam generating plant. The date is believed to be about 1920.

111 A major asset of the Frog-hall works was that it stood astride the Churnet Valley branch of the North Stafford-shire Railway. This provided the firm with an even faster means of distributing their products both to home markets, and to ports for export markets. Yet it is clear from the position of the steam generating plant (shown in this photograph) that it was always envisaged that coal slack would be delivered by boat, and this was done initially by owner-boatmen. Bolton's first boat *Lily of the Lake* was bought in 1908, followed by *Nora* in 1913 and *Beatrice* in 1916 (both named after the Bolton family), and *Havelock* in 1937. All these boats were horse-drawn and by 1953 all but *Beatrice* had been broken up, or sold. At this time *Beatrice* was 'still in use around the works'. Part of the Caldon Canal was dredged in an abortive attempt to restart this coal traffic during the winter of 1955-6.

112 Workmen unloading clay to repair a breach at Froghall,

about 1910. The narrow boat seen here is a forerunner of the modern work flat, and as this photograph shows, all loading and unloading had to be done by hand. The spades and wheel-barrow are of particular interest, being identical to those used by the original 'Navvies', as illus-trated in early prints. Ever since the Caldon Canal first opened, the stretch between Consall Mills and Froghall has suffered greatly

from landslips and breaches. Per-haps this says something of the ignorance of early canal engineers when it came to the geological structure of a particular area. However, in the case of this part of the canal, the confined valley floor and the meandering River Churnet presented them with few alternatives. Before the canal was restored, a section of the channel at Froghall was dammed and piped following a landslide.

112

113 The narrow boat *Edward*, one of the Brunner-Mond boats, entering the north-east portal of the Froghall Tunnel in 1902. The tunnel was not part of the original canal, as opened in 1778; but formed a section of a 540-yard extension which was constructed in the period 1783-5. Originally, the canal's terminal lay in the area beyond the south-west portal, which also marked the lower end of the first horse railway from the Cauldon Low quarries. The tunnel is 76yd long, and because there was no towing path, boats had to be 'legged' or 'shafted' through. The tunnel at Froghall pierces a steep sided spur, which shows up clearly in this photograph. A tunnel presented the only solution to an acute engineering problem, as a cutting here would have been impossible to maintain.

114 Froghall Tunnel during the restoration of the Caldon Canal. The brick invert arch is seen clearly.

115

115 A view of the approach to Froghall Wharf taken in 1905 from the bridge which carried the Moseymoor Brook tramway across the canal. The central wharf buildings serve as the main focus for this photograph, and as a background for two Brunner-Mond boats seen loading broken limestone in the entrance to Froghall Lock. Limestone was actually broken down to the required size on the canalside before being loaded into the boats, and the two sizes of limestone can be easily discerned. The boat in the foreground is another of those which belonged to Brunner-Mond, and is especially interesting as it clearly demonstrates the method of loading. The boats could carry about 20 tons of broken limestone, which was loaded into their holds in three heaps, the front two heaps being split by a box which usually contained horse feed. The drifting smoke is from the nearby limekilns.

116 A view taken from the white road bridge shown in the preceding photograph. It shows the innermost part of the basin at Froghall Wharf, around 1905. Here larger pieces of limestone were loaded either directly from tramway waggons (left), or from a great bank of limestone (right). One interesting point is that the boats were backed into this loading basin, like the empty boat shown in this photograph. Most of the limestone taken from Froghall by canal was intended for northerly markets, such as the ironworks of North Staffordshire and the Cheshire chemical works. That destined for South Staffordshire usually left by railway having been loaded on the tramway-railway interchange on the other side of the wharf area. There were exceptions to this rule and the boat nearest to the camera belonged to Price and Son, of Brierley Hill.

117 Froghall Wharf in 1905, a photograph which shows something of the cramped nature of the triangular site. The tramway-railway interchange is to the left of the central coal heap, and the boat loading area is to the right. Coal was brought in by rail and sometimes provided a return load for tramway waggons. Also to the right of the photograph is the lime tipple which loaded directly into boats, and was connected by a tramway to a shed where railway waggons were loaded with lime. The warehouse is also a prominent feature in this photograph, with its wooden loading bay sprung out over the canal from iron angle brackets. Alongside the warehouse, an interesting crane was located which was identical to the one used at Consall Mills. The huge lime-kilns at the wharf still survive, although it is clear that they were not the original ones erected by the canal company in 1786. Beyond the bridge was a brick-works and two kilns can be discerned.

118 The bearded gentleman in this photograph is John Billings who followed in his father's footsteps and became a platelayer on the Cauldon Low tramway. John began work for the North Staffordshire Railway Company in 1853 at the tender age of twelve; his first job being to help dismantle the 1802 tramroad which had been disused for four years by that time. He worked as a platelayer with his father on the 1849 line receiving wages of 2s 8d a day in 1869; and he continued to work in this capacity until he retired in February 1920 at the age of seventy-nine. In recognition of his sixty-seven years of service, the Traffic Committee of the Railway Company granted him a 'Retiring gratuity under very exceptional circumstances' of £25. A month after his retirement the tramway was closed and in May of the same year he died at Wharf House, Froghall.

119

119 The first horse-drawn railway from Froghall Basin to Cauldon Low opened in December 1778, but it appears to have been grossly inadequate and was described as being 'very crooked, steep and uneven in its degree of declivity, in different parts'. In 1785 the line was partially rebuilt with easier gradients and stretches of new line to avoid the worst sections of the old. Then in 1802 a new tramroad, incorporating four inclined planes was authorised according to a plan prepared by John Rennie. They were some of 'the most complete works of their kind in Britain'. However, by 1847 the demand for limestone was such that a replacement tramway was planned with four times the carrying capacity of the existing one and this was the line which opened in 1849. In this photograph a train of waggons is seen descending the tramway, below Harston Rock in 1905.

120

121

120 The 1849 line was heavily engineered but easy to operate as it ran practically dead straight with steadily rising gradients. It was divided into four sections, or inclines, each of which worked on the self-acting principle, a cable being wound around a drum at the top of each incline. In the middle of each incline there was a passing place for the waggons (as can be seen in the top photograph), which consisted of two lines of track, that is to say four rails. Above and below each passing place there were only three rails, the ascending and descending trains using a common middle rail. This

arrangement can be clearly seen in these photographs which were all taken on the Oldridge incline, in Harston Wood. Cleverly arranged pulley blocks and dumb blocks ensured that the steel cable never fouled passing waggons.

121 During the heyday of the line twelve brakesmen were employed to control the trains of waggons on the inclines and also to change the cables at the various stages. The trains were made up to a maximum of nine waggons, each carrying 6 tons of hand loaded limestone with some 1,000 tons being taken down

daily to Froghall Wharf. There were also two passenger cars, one enclosed and one open, and these were used to convey a party of North Staffordshire Railway officials up the line for the Coronation blast at the Cauldon quarries in 1902. The tramway also brought up coal to Cauldon Low as well as provisions for a small shop there. The line remained in regular use until 25 March 1920 when it was officially closed, although one informed source states that odd waggons of limestone were sent down to keep the limekilns at Froghall supplied until the contract with the operator lapsed.

122

123

122 This is a North Stafford-shire Railway Company official postcard of about 1905 showing the tramroad within the quarries at Cauldon Low. To the left are a couple of the special tank waggons which ran down empty to Garston to load water for the quarry engines. Traces of earlier quarry-ing can be seen in the shape of the low knolls which date from the late eighteenth century. When the Caldon Canal was proposed numerous small concerns were working the quarries and it was they who made agreements with the canal company. These pro-prietors were Thomas Gilbert, John Gilbert, Richard Hill, George Smith, Sampson Whiel-don, Henry Copestake, Henry Wooliscroft and Robert Bill. The company agreed to pay them 7d a ton for broken limestone and reserved the right to work the quarries themselves if the supply was not in keeping with their requirements.

123 Originally horses had been used for marshalling waggons into trains in the quarries and in 1869 seven horse-drivers were employed in this work. An out-break of influenza among the horses here and at Froghall Wharf in 1876 caused the North Staffordshire Railway Company to look at the possibilities of introducing locomotives. In the following year, two 0-4-0 saddle tank locomotives with outside cylinders and without cabs were bought from Henry Hughes & Co, of Loughborough. They were christened *Frog* and *Toad*. This photograph shows *Toad* in 1904 with quarrymen and empty waggons on the 3ft 6in gauge line. Although these engines took over the general quarry shunting and the marshalling of the trains for the cable line to Froghall, it is also clear from this photograph that they did not entirely replace horse haulage in the quarries.

124 Apparently satisfied with the performance of their two 3ft 6in gauge locomotives; the directors of the North Stafford-shire Railway Company ordered a third locomotive in 1901, to work in the Cauldon quarries. This locomotive was called *Bobs* after Field-Marshall, Lord Roberts VC, who had reinforced his own reputation and salvaged some national prestige from the Boer War. Built by W. J. Bagnall Ltd, of the Castle Engineering Works, Stafford it had the same wheel arrangement as the earlier loco-motives, with 7in × 12in cylinders and 2ft 3in wheels. Unlike the others, *Bobs* was built with a cut-down chimney and a dropped footplate and it is thought that this was to enable it to pass through a tunnel into another section of the quarry workings. All three quarry locomotives were taken from their sheds, still in their North Staffordshire Rail-way livery, and scrapped on the spot in May 1936. From 1904 the quarry was also served by a standard gauge line from Leek, so with the building of the 2ft 6in gauge Leek and Manifold Valley Light Railway the NSR had the distinction of being the only railway company in Britain to operate locomotives on three different gauges.

125 A party of North Staffordshire Railway officials at the
Cauldon Low quarries for the
1902 Coronation Blast. The 0-4-0
saddle tank engine *Toad* has just
brought the two special passenger
waggons from the top of the
inclines down to Froghall Wharf.
The bearded gentleman in the
bowler hat with his hands behind
his back is the legendary William
Douglas Phillipps, general
manager of the company from
1882 until 1917. After the opening of the Waterhouses branch
railway the Cauldon Low
quarries became a tourist
attraction, boasting a cave where
electricity was used to illuminate
stalactites and stalagmites. There
was another big blast at Cauldon
Low on 12 July 1938, detonated
by electricity from Euston
Station, London, and about
100,000 tons of limestone was
brought down, including the
foundation stone for the proposed new station. More recently
the Cauldon Low quarries have
supplied stone for the Thames
Barrage.

126 The north portal of the
tunnel on the Leek Canal, taken
in April 1964. When the route for
the Caldon Canal was finally
settled it effectively robbed Leek
of its proposed link with the
national canal network. This
proved to be a double blow
because there had been talk of an
independent company building a
canal to Leek; a survey had been
made and subscriptions collected
but the whole scheme was effectively squashed. So when in 1793
the canal company showed an
interest in using Rudyard Vale as
a reservoir, a number of the
townsfolk of Leek determined to
take advantage of the situation. A
feeder channel did not need to be
large to serve its purpose of
bringing down water from the
reservoir. But as a condition for
allowing the water to pass
through their land, some of the
landowners demanded that the
company should build a navigable
canal to Leek.

127 The company were also troubled by the rival Commercial Canal scheme at this time, and after their Rudyard Bill had been thrown out they agreed to build the branch canal to Leek. John Rennie made a final tour of inspection in March 1801 and shortly afterwards the Leek Canal was opened. The worst fears of the canal company were soon realised and traffic on the canal was never very significant, probably never reaching their 1797 estimate of ten boats a day. Coal was the most significant traffic and by 1834 the Woodhead Colliery Company had an agent at Leek Wharf. This unique photograph shows the wharf around 1900, about which time Henry de Salis wrote succinctly: 'There is not much traffic on this branch'. The small coal traffic from Norton ended in 1934, and a small tar trade from Leek to Milton in 1939, so the branch was abandoned in 1944.

128

128 Even though the Uttoxeter Canal had been abandoned for over sixty years, its top lock was still in use when this photograph was taken in 1910. Two Brunner-Mond boats can be seen loading up with limestone in Froghall lock, and another boat is moored in the basin below by a standard gauge railway spur. Beyond the line of the former canal was occupied by the railway. The Trent and Mersey Canal Company were in many ways forced to build a branch canal to Uttoxeter by the proposals for the rival Commercial Canal. This canal was intended to run from the Chester Canal at Nantwich to Sir Nigel Gresley's Canal, then across the Trent and Mersey Canal near Burslem and later the Caldon Branch, passing across the Cheadle coalfield before reaching Uttoxeter. From this point, it was to continue down the valley of the River Dove to cross the broad section of the Trent and Mersey Canal near Horninglow and then on to form a junction with the Ashby Canal.

129 Among the best examples of the standard of work demanded by John Rennie is this bricked-up bridge at Oakamoor, which carried the Blythe Marsh to Thorpe turnpike road over the Uttoxeter Canal. The bridge incorporates some fine stone-work by local masons who were often exasperated by the 'meticulous Mr. Rennie.' This photo-graph shows part of the area

known as Jimmy's Yard, once the wharf for the village of Oaka-moor. Beyond the bridge are the limekilns which were erected by John Leigh, principal partner in the Woodhead Colliery Com-pany and the North Stafford-shire Railway Company (1815-32). Work only began on the Uttoxeter Canal in 1806 and progress was slow, due to dis-putes over water supplies and a

and vested interests all served to ensure that it was the Trent and Mersey Canal Company who triumphed and in 1797 their Act passed through Parliament. When the Uttoxeter Canal was built the standard of the workmanship was exceptionally high as can be seen from the stonework of the derelict California Lock. John Farey was most impressed by the locks on this canal which had 'screws to draw the Lock-paddles, which stand a yard above the gates: the Lock-weirs are further from the Head-gates, and longer than usual.'

shortage of working capital. The stretch between Froghall and Oakamoor opened in August 1808.

130 During 1796 a great conflict arose between the Trent and Mersey Canal Company who put forward their rival Uttoxeter Canal scheme and the promoters of the Commercial Canal. Each side accused the other of underhand practices, including the publication of a hand-bill entitled 'Observations upon the Committee of Subscribers to the proposed Commercial Canal Scheme'. A combination of sharp practices, powerful connections

131 Minor alterations to the line of the canal had been brought about by a dispute between the Earl of Shrewsbury and the Cheadle Brass and Copper Company on the one hand and the canal company on the other. The Earl was concerned with the Churnet Valley being disfigured by the canal and the brass company were jealously guarding their water supply for their Alton brass wire mill. When the canal was opened to Oakamoor it benefited the Cheadle Brass and Copper Company who had another works there. Early in 1809, they purchased a narrow boat for transporting the company's goods to and from the new warehouse, which they had erected on the banks of the canal. This photograph shows the works in 1900 when they were owned by Thomas Bolton and Sons Ltd and known to the locals as the 'Smokeymoor works'. Another early user of the canal was the Woodhead Colliery Company, who had built a tramroad from their colliery (near Cheadle) to the Uttoxeter Canal at Eastwall, by 1809.

131

Bibliography

DIRECTORIES

Universal British Directory of Trade, Commerce and Manufacture, Volume II (1793)

W. Parson and T. Bradshaw, Staffordshire: General and Commercial Directory (1818)

White, Directory of Staffordshire (1834 and 1851)

BOOKS

Aikin, J., A Description of the Country from Thirty to Forty Miles Round Manchester (1795)

Baxter, Bertram, Stone Blocks and Iron Rails (Newton Abbot, 1966)

Bode, H., James Brindley (Aylesbury, 1973)

Boucher, C.T.G., James Brindley: Engineer (Norwich, 1968)

Brook, Fred, The Industrial Archaeology of the British Isles: The West Midlands (1977)

Christiansen, Rex, and Miller. R.W., The North Staffordshire Railway (Newton Abbot, 1971)

Cope, Norman A., Stone in Staffordshire: The History of a Market Town (Stone, 1972)

Copeland, Robert, A Short History of Pottery Raw Materials and the Cheddleton Flint Mill (Cheddleton, 1972)

Dendy Marshall, C.F., A History of British Railways Down To The Year 1830 (1938)

Farey, John, Agriculture and Minerals of Derbyshire (1817)

Farrer, E.F., Letters of Josiah Wedgwood (1903)

Hadfield, Charles, Canals of the West Midlands (Newton Abbot, 1969)

Hadfield, Charles, British Canals (Newton Abbot, 1974)

Hadfield, Charles, The Canal Age (Newton Abbot, 1968)

Hanson, Harry, The Canal Boatmen (Manchester, 1975)

Jeffery, Alan, The Caldon Canal (1971)

Johnstone, J.D., Werrington (1946)

Keys, Robert, The Churnet Valley Railway (Hartington, 1974)

Larking, R.M., The Canal Pioneers (Goring-by-Sea, 1967)

Lead, Peter, The Caldon Canal and Tramroads (Oakwood Press, 1979)

Lewis, M.J.T., Early Wooden Railways (1970)

Lindsay, J., The Trent and Mersey Canal (Newton Abbot, 1979)

Malet, Hugh, Bridgewater: The Canal Duke (Manchester, 1977)

Manifold, The North Staffordshire Railway (Ashbourne, 1952)

Mullineux, Frank, The Duke of Bridgewater's Canal (Eccles, 1959)

Priestley, Joseph, Navigable Rivers, Canals and Railways (1831)

Redfern, Francis, History of Uttoxeter (Hanley, 1886)

Rolt, L.T.C., Narrow Boat (London, 1944)

Rolt, L.T.C., Navigable Waterways (London, 1969)

De Salis, Henry, Bradshaw's Canals and Navigable Rivers (London, 1904)

Speake, Robert, The Old Road to Endon (Keele, 1974)

Ward, John, History of the Borough of Stoke-upon-Trent (1843)

ARTICLES

Beaver, S.H., 'The Potteries: A study in the Evolution of a Cultural Landscape', Trans Inst British Geographers, No 34 (1964)

Dodd, A.E. and E.M., 'Froghall-Uttoxeter Canal', North Staffs Journal of Field Studies, Vol 3 (1963)

Fell, M.G., 'Harecastle Tunnel Electric Tugs', Waterways World, June 1977

Hollick, J.R., 'The Caldon Low Tramways', Railway Magazine, June 1937

Jenkins, David and Lead, Peter, 'The Newcastle Canal', Six Towns Magazine, June 1972

Johnstone, J.D., 'The Consall Plateway', Railway Magazine, January/February 1949

Lead, Peter, 'Tramroads on the Potteries Coalfield', Journal of the Staffordshire Industrial Archaeology Society, 1974

Lead, Peter, 'The Proposed Inclined Plane at Newcastle-under-Lyme', Journal of the Railway and Canal Historical Society, Volume XX, No 3

Lead, Peter and Potts, B.A., 'Railway and Canals in the Apedale and Silverdale Valleys', Staffordshire Magazine, March 1973

Taylor, J.H., 'The Vestiges of the Newcastle-under-Lyme Canals', North Staffs Journal of Field Studies, Vol 13 (1973)

Roberts, Peter K., 'The Harecastle Electric Tugs', Journal of the Railway and Canal Historical Society, Volume XXIV, No 2

Index

These numbers refer to illustrations